BETHLEHEM

FADI KATTAN

CONTENTS

INTRODUCTION

Bethlehem: A city famous the world over, yet so often seen only through the eyes of the pilgrims passing through. A desire to show the real Bethlehem, and to celebrate it, is what led me to food and hospitality so many years ago. Cooking is how I tell Bethlehem's story.

Each recipe in this book contains memories of people, places, and moments in this city, from my childhood to my school years in Jerusalem, to my years abroad, and then my return home. Writing this book has also sent me back to memories of how the city has evolved under occupation, how the raising of walls has choked the livelihoods of many, how tourism has been subjected to ups and downs, how the visitors have come and gone. It has made me wonder how many Bethlehemites have returned back to their homes with stories
dating back thousands of years ago, carried in every dish, every spice, every cup of coffee.

Deciding to write about my Palestinian cuisine and share family stories, as well as celebrate some of the wonderful artisans of Bethlehem, felt natural, an extension of a discussion I would have with guests after their dinner at my restaurant Fawda in Bethlehem, or at Akub restaurant in London, or even at a conference in Toronto. These conversations encourage my guests in Bethlehem to walk the alleyways of the city and meet the people, and inspire others abroad to come to Bethlehem and share in the memories and flavours of a land far away.

Yalla! Take my hand and let's roam the stories and flavours of Bethlehem!

S P R I N G

BREAKFASTS WITH BABA FUAD

At a certain age, you start noticing habits that give you flashbacks to your childhood.

Increasingly these happen to me at breakfast, while I'm enjoying the simple pleasure of frying eggs for my family or laying out the table. Breakfast with my baba, my father, Fuad, was a ritual when I was young and still is today when we spend time together.

As a boy, I was always required to help with breakfast preparations, making sure that the coffee cups, plates, cutlery, and napkins were all set neatly in place. Then came the tray laden with zeit o zaatar—the winning combination of olive oil and a zaatar spice blend, some addictive thick and sticky dibs o tahinia (grape molasses mixed with sesame paste), and the crown jewels, homemade jams provided by Mama Micheline.

My father would always wake up before everybody else to squeeze the oranges when they were in season and receive a delivery of warm bread—white crusty loaves from the Salesian Bakery, round kmaj (pitas) from Al-Shweiki Bakery, or the wood-fire baked sesame ka'ek al-quds (see page 72). He would also take out the small dishes from the fridge that would have been prepared the night before—creamy labaneh (strained and seasoned yoghurt) and chunks of white Nabulsi cheese, covered in olive oil.

Then Baba would wake us up—probably as much of a tricky task with me today as it was in my youth. But the smell of eggs—fried or scrambled—and sometimes grilled bacon and sausages would soon summon me to the kitchen. Sometimes my father would smuggle a few slices of basturma into the house, the highly seasoned, cured Armenian beef that he and we children love so much but my mother abhors because of its strong fenugreek smell. I remember how he would have a friend bring it from an Armenian artisan in the Old City of Jerusalem and would hide it in the fridge until its scent gave its presence away, and we would have to gobble it up quickly.

Breakfast, with the family gathering together, was always a special way to start the day. We would sit and chat about our plans, share stories, and discuss everything amid the smell of toast and the taste of jam: apricot, Seville orange, strawberry, or quince—depending on the time of year. My father, a businessman, would often travel for work or have long, stressful days, but breakfast was a must. He swore by it and still does.

When my family discusses food and recipes, Baba is always first to confess that he is no cook and leaves the expertise of preparing elaborate Palestinian dishes to others. I often make fun if he tries to express an opinion on cuisine. However, my father may also point out that for years, he was the one to feed me at the start of each day, setting me up for whatever the day brought me. And at the start of each day, the kitchen remains—briefly—his domain.

TABOUN BREAD

1 tablespoon dry baker's
  yeast
½ teaspoon sugar
180 ml / ¾ cup warm
  water
250 g / 2 cups plus
  1 tablespoon all-
  purpose flour, plus
  more for the work
  surface
125 g / 1 cup whole
  wheat flour
½ teaspoon salt
1 tablespoon extra-virgin
  olive oil

**MAKES 4 TO 6
BREADS**

Taboun bread is one of the classic Palestinian breads. Traditionally, taboun is made in a special taboun oven, built with clay and hay, with an opening at the top to put the bread over stone pebbles. In Bethlehem, people would use olive wood and light up the taboun during the night, so in the morning, it would be hot. The ashes would be removed from around the oven and the inside would be ready for baking.

At my paternal grandparents' home, a taboun oven was outdoors on the balcony or on the terrace. At my maternal great-grandfather's home, there was a little stone hut outside that held a taboun. I still remember the smell of that burnt olive wood; it gave the taboun bread a very particular smoky scent.

However, with time, taboun ovens in the majority of homes stopped functioning or disappeared, and taboun makers have replaced them with modern technology. The best taboun rotary is found at Al-Shweiki Bakery. They have a round base of stone pebbles that turns around inside a gas oven. I replicate the same idea more or less at home: I take a baking sheet, fill it with clean washed pebbles, and preheat it in the oven before I lay down bread on top.

Key to baking the taboun was the tablecloth. There would always be an old cotton tablecloth to wrap the taboun breads in. Taboun bakers would place each fresh hot taboun into the folds of the tablecloth and slowly pile them up until they baked the last taboun bread. Covering the bread kept the steam in so the bread stayed soft.

In a small bowl, mix the yeast, the sugar, and a few tablespoons of the water and leave for 10 to 15 minutes, until it is bubbling.

In a mixing bowl or the bowl of a stand mixer fitted with a dough hook, combine the white and whole wheat flours, salt, olive oil, and yeast mixture. Slowly add the remaining water and mix the dough by hand or at low speed until the dough gets sticky.

Cover the dough and let rise for 1 hour, or until it doubles in size. In the cold months, it can take a longer time, between 1½ and 2 hours.

Once the dough is ready, press by hand to remove the gas in the risen dough, and then divide it into four to six portions.

Flour a work surface, add the portions of the dough, and cover them with a cloth to rise for another 30 to 45 minutes, or until the dough has nearly doubled in volume again.

Preheat the oven to 250°C / 475°F. Fill a baking sheet with clean pebbles and place on the bottom of the oven.

Roll out a portion of the dough on a floured surface, dust the dough with flour, and spread with your flour-dusted fingers into a circle about 15 cm / 6 inches in diameter. Flip it over while rolling it and stretching it, dusting your fingers and the dough as needed.

Place the dough on the hot pebbles and bake for 4 to 5 minutes, until coloured on the bottom. Then flip the bread and bake for another minute or so until it's coloured. Wrap the first taboun hot out of the oven with a cotton dish towel.

Return the pebbles to the oven and let heat until they are hot. Then repeat the steps with the dough to make the rest of the tabouns.

HOUMOUS MUTABAL BIL TAHINIA

This recipe is meant to celebrate the deliciousness of tahinia and chickpeas. Tahinia is produced from sesame seeds in the ancient factories of Palestine, from Jerusalem to Nablus, where a beautiful nutty scent emanates across the historic alleyways.

However, the essence of this dish is the chickpeas, or *hummus* in Arabic, not the variations that we are witnessing crop up across the world, where "hummus" seems to have become a term to describe any kind of dip with tahinia.

In Arabic, the word *mutabal* means "seasoned", but it describes so much more. Mutabal is seasoning with tahinia, fresh lemon juice, herbs, garlic, and spices which ends up being a mixture called *tatbileh*.

I call for almond slivers and sumac in the recipe, but parsley is a very good garnish too.

400 g / 14 ounces dried chickpeas, soaked overnight in water to cover
1 teaspoon baking soda
2 garlic cloves, crushed
250 g / ¾ cup plus 2 tablespoons tahinia
1 teaspoon salt
2 teaspoons ground cumin
Juice of 1 lemon
4 tablespoons extra-virgin olive oil, plus more to serve
1 tablespoon almond slivers
1 teaspoon ground sumac

SERVES 8

Drain the chickpeas and combine them in a saucepan with the baking soda and 1¼ L / 5 cups water. Bring to a boil over high heat and then decrease the heat to medium-low and simmer for 30 minutes, until the chickpeas are soft throughout. While cooking, regularly remove the foam that can float on top.

Drain the chickpeas, reserving the cooking water. Reserve a few chickpeas for decorating the dish and transfer the rest to a mixing bowl. Use a hand-held blender at low speed to crush the chickpeas into a paste. Add the garlic cloves and continue blending. Slowly add the tahinia, salt, cumin, and lemon juice while blending. Add 4 tablespoons of the chickpea cooking water while blending. If the paste is not smooth, you may need to add up to 1 more tablespoon.

Using a large spoon or a spatula, gently fold in 3 tablespoons of the olive oil until you obtain a creamy, silky consistency.

In a small pan, heat the remaining 1 tablespoon of olive oil over medium heat. Add the almond slivers and fry until lightly coloured, about 2 minutes. Drain on paper towels.

Transfer the houmous to a plate and sprinkle the reserved chickpeas, the almonds, and sumac on top. Drizzle with a little olive oil and serve.

BETHLEHEM

EGGS IN SAMNEH WITH SUMAC

Perhaps my earliest childhood food memory is of sitting at the table in my grandmother Julia's kitchen, watching her crack the eggs in the bubbling samneh (ghee) and slowly using the spoon to baste the egg whites, while taking care to leave the golden yolks runny. She would then slide the eggs onto a plate and sprinkle them with sumac and salt.

I recall anticipating that first dip of fresh bread into the runny egg yolks, that first taste of the creamy eggs, and the tang of the sumac.

1 tablespoon samneh
    (ghee)
4 eggs
1 generous pinch of
    ground sumac
1 pinch of salt

SERVES 2

Heat the samneh (ghee) in a pan over medium-high heat until liquid and bubbly. Crack the eggs into the pan and leave to cook until the egg whites are set, 3 minutes. With a spoon, slowly baste the egg whites until the sides are crispy.

Serve on two plates, sprinkled with sumac and salt.

HWERNEH
IN
LABANEH

The first *hwerneh* (mustard greens) of the season that grows in Palestine comes from Jericho, an oasis city that is much warmer than the rest of the country and is dotted with natural springs. Hwerneh, macerated and fermented in yoghurt is full of creamy sunshine. An ideal dip for breakfast, lunch, or dinner. I played around with the recipe, replacing the yoghurt with labaneh—strained and seasoned yoghurt—for deeper flavour.

2 bunches mustard greens
1 tablespoon coarse sea
    salt, plus more to taste
720 ml / 3 cups labaneh
1 tablespoon extra-virgin
    olive oil, to serve
Bread, such as kmaj or
    taboun, to serve

SERVES 8

Strip the leaves from the coarse stems of the mustard and discard the stems. You can leave the thin soft stems. On a chopping board, lay the leaves one over the other and chop them to make thin strips. Put the chopped leaves in a colander, add the salt, and rub it into the leaves. Place the colander in a bowl, refrigerate, and allow to drain for at least 6 hours and up to overnight.

Squeeze the wilted chopped leaves to remove any remaining liquid and place in a mixing bowl. Add the labaneh and salt to taste. Mix well and store in a glass jar in the fridge for at least 3 days and up to 10 days to ferment.

Serve on a plate, drizzled with olive oil. Serve bread alongside for scooping.

THE QUEEN OF HERBS AND HER ANCIENT VILLAGE

As a child, I would often go with my grandparents to the picturesque Canaanite village of Artas, which lies in a lush green valley just south of Bethlehem. As we would drive across the stone bridge to reach a well-known convent there, I always enjoyed the stunning view of the land, carefully tended by local families and rich in produce, most famously, grapes and lettuces.

My grandparents liked to visit the sisters of the Convent of the Hortus Conclusus ("Enclosed Garden"), and we would picnic amidst the natural beauty of its grounds. Sometimes we would play under the trees, close to the ancient Solomon's Pools. It is said that in Artas, King Solomon wrote the "Song of Songs", the biblical text celebrating carnal beauty and love.

For me, as for most Bethlehemites, Artas is synonymous with fine herbs, succulent fruits, and crunchy vegetables. I can still recall my delight as a boy, biting into one of its freshly picked lettuces.

For more than four decades now, Um Nabil, a native of Artas, has headed from her small village into Bethlehem's Old City early every day, except Fridays, carrying its riches to our souk. She is there through the chills of winter and the parched, hot days of summer. First, as a young woman, she sold milk and cheese that she and her husband produced. Later, after they sold their cows, she began to offer seasonal produce grown by her neighbours or brought to her by small farmers and foragers.

Um Nabil, always dressed in a traditional embroidered Palestinian robe, sits regally in her established spot, on the steps at the entrance of the market, where

she displays her fresh herbs and vegetables tantalisingly around her. I call her the "Queen of Herbs".

For me, as a young food lover, she had an almost mythical status. When taken shopping, I would constantly hear her name referenced, with one person telling another "Get the *silek* (chard) from Um Nabil" or "Um Nabil has superb wild zaatar today".

Fast forward a few years, to when I moved back to my family home in the Old City and opened my restaurant nearby. It was inevitable that Um Nabil, with her warm smile and encyclopaedic knowledge of Palestinian food, would become a fixture of my daily life.

I tend to start my mornings dropping by her stall to chat and check out the mouthwatering produce she has that day. From fragrant zaatar to fat turnips, from finger-length, hot chillies to tender, fresh grape leaves (*warak dawali*), all the regular fare tastes better from her stall than anyone else's. But then, there is always a little surprise, a foraged delicacy lying in wait for me. Sometimes it is *hwerneh* (*Sisymbrium officinale*), or mustard greens. Sometimes we gather loof (*Arum palaestinum*), also known as black calla, Solomon's lily, priest's hood, and kardi. Um Nabil teases me when she sees my purchase by asking "So, what

are you going to do with it?" Often, a visit to her stall inspires my menu for the day, totally reshaping the ideas that had been forming in my head.

At the same time, my conversations with Um Nabil and the changing goods on her stall are a reminder of the realities of agriculture in the Bethlehem area. Nowadays, the land of Artas is less and less cultivated. A young generation of Palestinians are leaving farming either for more comfortable jobs in the Palestinian public sector or well-paid construction work in Israel. Um Nabil and I often discuss the impact of these changes on farming but also the horrendous conditions the remaining workers have to go through, leaving home at the crack of dawn, queuing at illegal occupation checkpoints, confronting random and arbitrary policies. Knowledge of the land is rapidly being lost. Water is another huge problem. The verdant valley of Artas is drying up as expanding Israeli settlements encroach on nearby hilltops and divert the water that used to flow down naturally and nourish its springs.

Her eyes tear up when she talks about Christian–Muslim relations in Bethlehem, a subject we both have close to heart and are proud of. In discussions about her friends and experiences, she shares stories of Bethlehem; the bonds between people of different faiths, between people from the city, the villages, and the refugee camps. She always finishes that chapter of our discussions with: "God bless the people! God bless the people of Palestine! May nothing ever divide us!"

Um Nabil is stoic and the embodiment of what we call in Arabic *sumood,* or resilience. She has seen it all: the Palestinian intifadas, or uprisings, the incursions by Israeli troops in Bethlehem, the storms, the heat waves, and the coronavirus pandemic. Yet she remains a constant presence in the Old City, with her dignified, friendly manner and top-quality produce, ready to bring flavour to each day.

We often discuss recipes and talk about local characters, comparing the present and the past. Um Nabil always has advice for the best way to serve what she sells, and she looks at me doubtfully when I say that I fry the leaves of molokhia (*Corchorus olitorius*; also called Egyptian spinach or jute mallow) or use her fresh chamomile in a delicious salad. She is proud of her reputation and the excellent produce she sells and of being a stalwart of the historic market, sharing her love for Palestinian food and the land with everyone, whether they are regular customers, tourists, or simply passersby.

CHEESE-STUFFED GRAPE LEAVES

This recipe is inspired by my mother's moreish meat kofta in grape leaves. By substituting Akkawi or Nabulsi cheese for the meat, it makes an easy starter, perfect for vegetarians. Grape leaves are a key ingredient in Palestinian cuisine. They are usually rolled and stuffed with meat and rice, or just rice and herbs, or are wrapped around meat patties. I am always impressed at the speed and expertise of Palestinian women as they roll the leaves into piles of delicious, tiny parcels.

Both Akkawi and Nabulsi are fresh cheeses stored in brine. The mixture in the grape leaves includes the perennial herb zaatar. You may know zaatar as a spice blend, but it is also an herb, also called *Origanum Syriacum*.

CHEESE PARCELS

20 fresh grape leaves (or substitute leaves stored in a brine)
1 tablespoon raisins
Olive oil, for brushing
150 g / 5¼ ounces Akkawi or Nabulsi cheese (or substitute another fresh brined cheese, such as halloumi, fresh Syrian cheese, or queso blanco)
2 small tomatoes, thinly sliced
3 tablespoons dried and crumbled zaatar leaves (or substitute oregano)

DRESSING

2 tablespoons extra-virgin olive oil
1 pinch of salt
Leaves of 5 sprigs of fresh mint or fresh zaatar, or other green herb of choice
2 drops of water (optional)

SERVES 10

To make the parcels, if you're using fresh grape leaves, blanch the whole leaves in a large pot of lightly salted water until they turn a deep green and are soft to the touch, 5 to 7 minutes, depending on the thickness of the leaves. Drain well.

Put the raisins in a bowl filled with enough warm water to cover them, because we need to hydrate them slightly.

Brush ten little ramekins, 5 to 7 cm / 2 to 3 inches in diameter, with a bit of olive oil. Place two grape leaves in each one, with the top side downwards so that when we flip the ramekin, we'll end up with the outside of the leaves facing up.

Cut the cheese into ten equal portions. Drain the raisins.

Put one piece of cheese, a slice of tomato, a few raisins, and a bit of zaatar leaves on the grape leaves. Fold the leaves to enclose the filling in the ramekins.

Preheat the oven to 160°C / 325°F. Place the ramekins in a roasting pan and fill the pan with water to the height of the grape leaves in the ramekins. Cover the top of the ramekins with a baking sheet; we don't want the grape leaves to dry out.

Bake for 20 minutes. Remove the ramekins from the water bath and let cool.

When you're ready to serve, flip the ramekins onto plates to see the beautiful stuffed grape leaves.

To make the dressing, combine the olive oil, salt, and herbs in a blender and process to a homogenous green sauce. Add the water to thin the dressing, if needed. Sprinkle it on top of the grape leaves and serve.

BETHLEHEM

LAMB SHANKS

This recipe is inspired by mansaf, a dish made of lamb cooked in a sauce of laban jameed, a fermented dried yoghurt, and served with rice or wheat bulgur. I have a passion for laban jameed which embodies Palestinian umami. It comes from the dairy culture of the desert, where yoghurt is preserved and dried with sun and salt. It adds a beautiful flavour to meats, rice, or vegetables. I use laban jameed in many different dishes, often grating it over lamb, salads, and freekeh. Whatever way, it's fabulously delicious.

1 ball laban jameed, about 250 g / 9 ounces
500 ml / 2 cups water
1 onion, cut in half
2 cinnamon sticks
4 bay leaves
6 cardamom pods
4 lamb shanks, 250 to 300 g / 9 to 10 ounces each
1 tablespoon extra-virgin olive oil
3 garlic cloves, crushed, plus 3 garlic cloves, thinly sliced
80 g / 2¾ ounces peeled (blanched) almonds
80 g / 2¾ ounces pistachios
80 g / 2¾ ounces pine nuts

SERVES 4

The night before, reserve about 50 g / 1¾ ounces of the laban jameed ball for plating, and soak the rest in water overnight.

Fill a large pot with the water and add the onion, cinnamon sticks, bay leaves, cardamom, and lamb. Bring to a boil over medium-high heat. Decrease the heat and remove any foam that forms on the surface of the water. Simmer for about 2 hours, until the meat is tender but still holding onto the bone.

Remove the meat from the broth and let rest for 10 minutes, saving 240ml / 1 cup of meat broth.

Drain the laban jameed that has been soaking overnight.

In a separate pot, heat 1½ teaspoons of the olive oil over medium heat. Add the crushed garlic and cook for 30 seconds, until fragrant. Add the soaked laban jameed and 240 ml / 1 cup of the meat broth. Cook over medium heat, whisking, until the laban jameed dissolves into a warm, smooth sauce.

In a small pan, heat the remaining 1½ teaspoons of olive oil over medium heat. Add the sliced garlic and fry until it becomes lightly coloured, about 1 minute. Remove the garlic and set aside, then fry the nuts until they turn golden, 2 to 3 minutes.

To serve, into four wide bowls, spoon some jameed sauce. Place the lamb shank on top, then sprinkle on the garlic and golden nuts. Grate the reserved laban jameed over the meat or use a knife to make thin shavings to sprinkle on top.

PICKLED GREEN ALMONDS

The beginning of spring in Palestine is a time to celebrate the almond. We do not wait for them to ripen and harden; we pick the first batches while they are still green and tender. They are sold on carts by street vendors for people to munch, dipped in salt. We pickle them to preserve their green freshness and we also dry the almonds and use them or as salted roasted almond snacks.

1¾ L / 7⅓ cups water
60 g / ½ cup salt
500 g / 18 ounces green almonds
250 ml / 1 cup white wine vinegar
2 sprigs rosemary
6 white peppercorns
4 cardamom pods
2 garlic cloves, finely chopped

MAKES 1 L / 4¼ CUPS

Mix 1½ L / 6⅓ cups of the water and the salt in a large saucepan to make the brine. Bring to a boil over medium heat, stirring to dissolve the salt. Then remove from the heat.

Wash the almonds under running water. Then pierce the almonds from top to bottom with a metal skewer, to allow the brine to soak in. Drop the almonds into the brine and allow to soak overnight.

In another pot, mix together the remaining 240 ml / 1 cup water, the vinegar, rosemary, peppercorns, cardamom, and garlic. Bring to a boil over medium heat, remove from the heat, cover, and allow the aromatics to infuse the liquid overnight.

The next morning, remove the almonds from the brine, rinse them, and place them in sterilized jars.

Bring the vinegar mixture to a boil and pour over the almonds, covering them entirely.

Seal the jars well and allow to cool before refrigerating. The pickled almonds can be eaten after one week and will keep, refrigerated, for up to two months.

ARAYES
SHRAK

250 g / 9 ounces
  ground beef
250 g / 9 ounces
  ground lamb
1 onion, finely chopped
1 green chilli, finely
  chopped
2 garlic cloves, finely
  chopped
20 g / ½ cup finely
  chopped fresh flat-leaf
  parsley
1 teaspoon salt
½ teaspoon ground
  allspice
½ teaspoon ground
  coriander
½ teaspoon ground cumin
¼ teaspoon ground black
  pepper
4 shrak breads (or
  substitute lavash,
  markook, or any thin
  bread)
1 tablespoon extra-virgin
  olive oil
1 cube of lamb fat, 20 to
  50 g / ¾ to 1¾ oz

MAKES 8 ARAYES

The best arayes (stuffed pitas) in Palestine are made in the old city of Nablus, a bustling food haven in the north of the West Bank. I always go to the best baker in the Old City, Al-Wawi, to get half-baked pita breads, and then head to Bashar Al-Masri's butcher shop, where they make the best arayes in town. The butcher expertly minces the meat in front of you, fills the pita, and bakes it in an oven, just until it is crispy. Then he takes it out and rubs a piece of lamb fat, called *liyyeh*, on the hot arayes and gives them a last browning bake in the oven.

For the full experience, walk a bit further into the Old City, stop by the Al-Amad pickle shop, and get a variety of colourful pickles to enjoy with your arayes.

For this recipe, instead of using a pita, I use shrak, a thin round bread that can be rolled to make arayes. Enjoy these with yoghurt, tahinia, or a spicy dip on the side and plenty of pickles.

In a bowl, combine the beef, lamb, onion, chilli, garlic, parsley, salt, allspice, coriander, cumin, and pepper and mix by hand until evenly combined.

On a work surface, spread a shrak flat and cut it in half. Fill a half-circle of bread with 1 tablespoon of the minced meat and roll it to get a cigar-shaped araye. Repeat with the remaining shrak.

Preheat a gas or charcoal barbecue (grill) to medium-high heat or a skillet over medium-high heat. Brush the grill rack or skillet with olive oil, add the arayes and cook for 5 to 6 minutes on each side, until the outside is crispy and the filling is cooked.

Before you remove the arayes from the heat, rub a square of fat on both sides of the arayes and cook for another minute on all sides. Remove from the heat and serve.

BETHLEHEM BAKERIES

Bread is such an essential part of Palestinian cuisine. We do not just make it into sandwiches, we learn to use it expertly to dip into and scoop up food such as houmous. It forms the tasty base of favourite dishes, such as mansaf (lamb cooked in a sauce of laban jameed) and musakhan (chicken roasted with onions and sumac and served over taboun bread). And no steaming bowl of lentil soup or molokhia (*Corchorus olitorius* or jute leaves) is complete without crunchy fried bread—our local version of croutons.

All around Bethlehem, you will still find independent bakeries. In times of crisis or a general strike, these are among the only shops you will routinely find open. Inevitably, there are some that are sought out for the particular breads they supply, but there are also several that I have a special connection to. The smells and distinctive shapes and qualities of their freshly baked loaves, as well as the characters who bake and sell them, are part of the fabric of our everyday lives.

The most commonly consumed bread is a circular, leavened, double-layered one that seems to have its origins in the prehistoric flatbreads of the wider region. It is called pita internationally, but in the Palestinian dialect, it is known as *kmaj*. This you will find baked fresh each morning all over the city, in the prominent, main bakeries and other stores which buy from them. You will see boys balancing long trays of it precariously on their heads, often using a small round cushion. The bread, sold in packs of ten, is a staple of every Palestinian home.

When I am traveling overseas, after a time, I will always crave Bethlehem's kmaj. Specifically, I long for the Al-Shweiki Bakery on the main road towards the Nativity Church. As a child, I would regularly stop off there in the evenings with my aunt Pauline and uncle George whom I often visited after school, asking for help with tricky subjects such as algebra. There was such a delight in driving around town with them, munching on a scalding-hot piece of kmaj. For me, this loaf still has the perfect measure of slight saltiness. The only downside of Shweiki's kmaj has been that it has ruined forever the possibility of my being able to enjoy any other pita-type bread, wherever it is from.

The Shweiki family also owns a small, older bakery right in the middle of Bethlehem's bustling market, the old souk. This bakery distinguishes itself

by making two traditional types of Palestinian bread, taboun (see page 16) and shrak. Both are delicious in their own right but are also essential parts of favourite dishes. Now that bread is less routinely made at home, those of us living nearby and wanting to make mansaf or musakhan are obliged to pay a visit to Abu Hussein, the friendly, bald-headed baker who works with Ayman Shweiki and is constantly shuttling between the shop window and the wondrous oven operating in the shadows behind him.

Taboun is a larger, round, flattish whole wheat bread that is baked in a round, wood-fired clay oven with a cooking surface of stones from the sea, which helps give it a special taste and rougher texture. In fact, a lot of older homes, including mine, have a little shack outside where the taboun used to be, a small oven dug into the wall or built on the floor for the fire and stones. Baking the taboun can only begin once the fire is fully alight and the stones have become charged with heat. Then the ball of dough is flattened and laid down, covered, then flipped to produce the taboun bread. Nowadays, there are hazards and time constraints that make this style of home baking less appealing. However, at the Al-Shweiki bakery, they have invented a way of safely and efficiently producing larger quantities. They have a machine that is gas fuelled, with a rotating stone bed that goes into the oven to make their excellent loaves.

Taboun is typically larger than a dinner plate and is used as the base of musakhan, one of our Palestinian national dishes, which is often made to celebrate the new olive oil season. The bread is drenched lavishly in olive oil— greenish or golden—with grilled chicken just visible beneath a heap of purple sumac and onions. Once assembled, the whole dish is heated briefly in the oven before it is topped off with a sprinkling of pine nuts. As soon as it is served, you dig in, ripping off pieces of the taboun bread, textured perfectly to absorb the olive oil, so that each mouthful drips with it deliciously.

Shrak is a less filling variety of bread. It is very thin, like a crêpe, but surprisingly strong and versatile, made with a mixture of whole and white wheat flour. It is baked on a hot metal dome called a *saj*, so that the bread is sometimes called *saj* or *sajia* (or *tava* in an Indian market). The saj is a common feature outside a Palestinian bakery, where you will often see a young man skillfully producing these tray-sized breads. The dough is stretched over a round pillow and then transferred to the top of the saj, where it bakes very quickly. It is then carefully turned over onto the pillow so that it does not break. The result is a fine, silky, and malleable bread.

One of my favourite fast snacks is a shrak sandwich, the bread loaded up with labaneh (strained and seasoned yoghurt) and zaatar, then rolled into a thin, long sandwich. Shrak can also be used to serve shawarma or grilled meats. Then there are traditional dishes that are built around it, such as fatteh, created with layers of bread, meat, eggplant, or houmous all buried under a generous portion of garlic yoghurt and topped with pieces of fried bread. For mansaf, we pile the boiled lamb meat and rice coated in steaming, thick, salty laban jameed (see page 33) onto a shrak, then sprinkle roasted sliced almonds on the top. The dish can then be eaten efficiently in a Bedouin style with your fingers, each mouthwatering ball of rice and meat held in a small piece of shrak.

Closer to home, the Salesian Bakery is laden with special significance for me. It is run by the Salesian Convent and Church, which have a large compound by the entrance of the Old City of Bethlehem. The Salesian congregation is a Catholic order with a mission to help the young and the poor, with education in particular. In Bethlehem, in the late nineteenth century, it opened an orphanage followed by the Salesian Technical School, which went on to provide vocational training, such as carpentry, blacksmithing, and other crafts. My family were evidently dedicated customers as many treasured pieces of furniture in our home were made by the school's artisans, including the dining table. At breakfast time, that table will usually be graced with a selection of breads from the Salesian Bakery.

The Salesian Bakery makes white loaves that are not traditional but have become well-known in Bethlehem. One of its favourite innovations is the oval bread popularly known as *hamam*—or dove—which is crusty with a thick inside. There is also a long baguette-type shape and the shorter roll version, *sammun*. This can easily be cut up and made into sandwiches but I love to grill it and dip it into labaneh. There is also a small, round zaatar bread, flavoured with dried zaatar leaves. The bakery opens very early each day and often closes by 9 am. There is a constant stream of people rushing into the bakery to carry off the fresh, warm loaves.

It is not just the taste of the bread from the Salesian Bakery which I appreciate, it is the philosophy of their convent and church, too, which is upheld through the businesses and institutions which they establish. They help the community in a respectful and humble way, distributing bread to needy families regardless of their religion, origins, or back stories. For me it represents the essence of solidarity and community responsibility.

My final favourite bakery is a small place called Abu Fuad, which makes ka'ek al-quds (see page 72), the sesame seed–coated bread that so represents Jerusalem but which is also made in every Palestinian town. At Abu Fuad, there is an impressively large wood-fired oven used to cook the loops of sticky bread dough. It is mesmerising to watch the baker expertly use his long-handled wooden peel to slide out the baked loaves. The smell is heavenly, too, ensuring that queuing for your hot loaves is never tiresome.

What I especially like about Abu Fuad is that they also bake eggs slowly in the wood fire, giving them a yellow colour when you peel off the shell and a delicious, smoky taste. They also offer a large, chewy kind of falafel. These are served with a particularly salty zaatar which makes for an excellent breakfast.

I love to collect the bread for weekend breakfasts with my father, but when I am feeling too lazy to make it to the ka'ek oven, there is always another option. All around Bethlehem, you will hear the ka'ek sellers—local personalities who sell the bread, eggs, falafel, and zaatar from small wooden carts which they push around the busy streets. Their cries of "ka'ek, ka'ek" always set my stomach rumbling, convincing me of a hitherto unacknowledged need for this amazing bread. Once they have my attention, each ka'ek seller has a gift of persuading me to buy more bread than I had ever guessed that I needed.

MUJADARA

When I close my eyes and try to think of a dish that says home, many appear. Mujadara is one of them. At the beginning of the pandemic, when I started my radio show, *Sabah Al-Yasmine, Ramblings of a Chef,* the recipe most requested by people locked up in their homes across the world was mujadara, a humble but satisfying meal.

It is worth noting that there are probably as many variations of mujadara as there are Palestinians.

280 g / 10 ounces green
    lentils
½ teaspoon salt
125 ml / ½ cup extra-
    virgin olive oil
4 red onions, halved and
    thinly sliced
Salt
1 teaspoon sugar
1 teaspoon ground cumin
1 teaspoon ground
    coriander
1 teaspoon ground
    cinnamon
350 g / 1¾ cups medium-
    grain rice
600 ml / 2½ cups hot
    water

DRESSING
2 spring onions (scallions,
    chopped)
Juice of 2 lemons
1 teaspoon ground sumac
1 teaspoon extra-virgin
    olive oil

SERVES 4

Soak the lentils in water to cover for 30 minutes. Drain and discard the soaking water.

In a pot, combine the lentils, salt, and 750 ml / 3⅛ cups water. Cook over medium heat until the lentils are al dente, 10 to 12 minutes. Drain in a colander, rinse the lentils with cold water to stop the cooking, then leave to drain.

Pour 60 ml / ¼ cup of the olive oil into a medium-size frying pan over medium heat. Add the onions and sprinkle with a pinch of salt. Cover and cook over low heat for 3 to 4 minutes, until translucent. Sprinkle the sugar on the onions and cook for 6 to 8 more minutes, until the onions are caramelised.

Drain half the onions on paper towels and leave the other half in the oil.

In a large pot, heat the remaining 60 ml / ¼ cup of olive oil over medium-high heat. Stir in the cumin, coriander, cinnamon, and ½ teaspoon salt. Stir well until the spices release their fragrance, about 2 minutes. Add the rice, stir well to coat with the spices, then pour in the hot water. Bring to a boil and decrease the heat to medium. Cook for 4 to 5 minutes. Add the lentils and stir well. Continue to cook until the lentils and rice are tender with a slight crunch—almost done, about 12 minutes.

Pour the reserved onions and oil into the pot, stir well to mix with the rice and lentils, and leave on low heat until the water reduces. Turn off the heat and keep the pot covered for 10 minutes.

Meanwhile, to make the dressing, combine the spring onions, lemon juice, sumac, and remaining 1 teaspoon of olive oil. Transfer the rice and lentils to a serving bowl and fluff with a fork. Sprinkle the dressing on top. Garnish with the reserved caramelised onions and serve.

SAYADIEH SAMAK

2 kg / 4½ pounds whole
    sea bass
2 teaspoons salt
Juice of 1 lemon
500 ml / 2 cups vegetable
    oil, for frying
1 cinnamon stick
3 bay leaves
5 cardamom pods
4 onions, halved and thinly
    sliced
2 tablespoons all-purpose
    flour
1 teaspoon ground cumin
1 teaspoon ground allspice
½ teaspoon ground
    turmeric
½ teaspoon ground
    nutmeg
600 g / 3 cups long-grain
    rice
75 ml / 5 tablespoons
    extra-virgin olive oil
50 g / ⅓ cup almond
    slivers
50 g / ⅓ cup pine nuts

SERVES 6

Sayadieh evokes memories of the beaches of Gaza and lunches at the homes of my relatives. Or, before the blockade of this tiny strip of land, at one of the Gaza restaurants. It also evokes memories of my family in Jaffa and my cooking series, *Teta's Kitchen*. For one particularly memorable episode, I prepared sayadieh, a dish of fish and rice, with Nadia Chacar, a Palestinian from Jaffa, who had the graciousness to send a fish to me in Bethlehem. We cooked together over a Zoom call, as I was not able to visit her. I like to think of sayadieh as the coastal Palestinian equivalent of makloubeh, a layered dish of lamb and rice. Despite the differences between the two, both are such staples.

Fillet the sea bass and reserve the bones and heads.

Marinate the fillets in 1 teaspoon of the salt and the lemon juice. Set aside.

Fill a pan for deep-frying with 200 ml / ¾ cup of the vegetable oil and heat over high heat to 180°C / 350°F. Add the fish bones and heads and fry until they're brown on both sides, about 10 minutes total. Remove from the oil with a slotted spoon and drain on paper towels. Set the pan aside.

Fill a pot with 1 L / 4½ cups water. Add the cinnamon stick, bay leaves, cardamom pods, remaining 1 teaspoon salt, and fried fish bones and heads. Bring to a boil over high heat. Decrease the heat and simmer for about 20 minutes, until the broth is flavorful.

In the same pan used for frying the fish bones, reheat the oil to 180° C / 350° F. Add the onions and fry until they're caramelised, 15 to 20 minutes. While they're cooking, sprinkle with a pinch of salt. Drain on paper towels.

Strain the broth and discard the bones and the spices.

In a bowl, mix the flour, cumin, allspice, turmeric, and nutmeg. Dredge both sides of each fillet in the flour mixture.

Heat the remaining 300 ml / 1¼ cups vegetable oil in a clean frying pan over high heat to 180°C / 350°F. Add the fillets in batches and fry on both sides until they're cooked through and golden, about 6 minutes per side.

Rinse and drain the rice.

In a large pot, layer the onions, the fish, and the rice. Pour in the broth and cover the pot with the lid. Cook over high heat until the broth boils, then decrease the heat and leave it to cook until the rice is cooked through and tender, about 25 minutes.

Meanwhile, in a small frying pan, heat the olive oil over medium heat. Fry the almonds for 3 minutes. Add the pine nuts and fry until they're golden, 1 minute more. Set aside on paper towels.

When the rice is done, remove the lid and flip the pot onto a serving tray. You'll end up with layers of fried fish and caramelised onions. Sprinkle the almonds and pine nuts on top and serve.

SLOW-ROASTED LAMB

Lamb is the meat you cook in Palestine to honour a guest. From the feasts of mansaf to the roasted stuffed lambs in the tannurs of the Samaritans, lamb is always the pièce de résistance of a Palestinian celebration table.

Fenugreek is widely used in Palestine in a dessert cake made of semolina called hilbeh, and rarely in a savoury preparation. In this recipe, fenugreek, cardamom, and allspice lend the succulent lamb a delicious fragrance.

2 teaspoons cardamom pods
1½ teaspoons fenugreek seeds
1½ teaspoons allspice berries
2 teaspoons coarse sea salt, plus more as needed
2 tablespoons extra-virgin olive oil
2¼ kg / 4½ pounds whole bone-in leg of lamb
1 garlic bulb, halved
2 onions, quartered
500 ml / 2⅛ cups lamb stock (or substitute chicken stock)

SERVES 4 TO 6

Preheat the oven to 220°C / 425°F.

Slightly crush the cardamom pods with the blunt end of a knife and place in a bowl. Add the fenugreek, allspice, salt, and olive oil and mix well. Rub it all over the leg of lamb.

Transfer the lamb to a roasting pan and roast for 20 minutes, until browned. Remove the pan from the oven and decrease the heat to 160°C / 325°F.

Add the garlic, onions, and lamb stock to the roasting pan. If the lamb is not one-quarter submerged in the liquid, add some hot water. Cover the roasting pan first with parchment paper, then aluminum foil.

Cook for 3½ hours. Check the liquid, add more hot water as needed, and return the pan to the oven for another 2½ hours. The lamb should be falling apart. Uncover and roast for 20 minutes more to brown.

Remove the lamb from the oven, cover with parchment paper, then aluminum foil, and let rest for 20 minutes.

Transfer the lamb to a cutting board. Pass the pan juices through a fine-mesh sieve into a small saucepan, discarding the solids. Simmer the juices over medium heat to reduce to a thick sauce, around 15 minutes, then taste and add salt if needed. Serve the lamb with a spoonful of the sauce on top.

JERICHO

Jericho is a small town a few miles from the Dead Sea, the lowest point on earth. It's an oasis with water-rich canals that run through the city. Tiny canals, which I grew up playing in, transport water to properties across Jericho. The canals irrigate the orange plantations and other farms. On the outskirts of the city, you can see the palm plantations; they require less water. The available water from the springs allows different herbs to grow all over the area during spring and autumn.

Jericho is usually a winter vacation destination for people from the West Bank. The weather is mild and warm, a nice change away from higher areas, which are usually much colder in winter. When I was a child, there wasn't as much construction as there is today. Nowadays people build villas around Jericho as winter vacation homes or to be rented out for a couple of days. My grandparents would often spend time in Jericho, and we would join them on Sundays, the day that is always reserved for family. We would play in the garden surrounding the rented house, and go down the valley to pick herbs or to a nearby orange farm to pick fruit.

There are many herbs that grow in Jericho. In my memory I link Jericho to *hwerneh*, mustard greens, a very sharp-tasting herb. We would pick branches of hwerneh from fields that are close by. We'd chop it, add yoghurt, and let it ferment to use as a dip (see page 22). The Arab Development Project was established by friends of my grandparents, and it was the first industrial Palestinian farm to be mainly financed by dairy operations, including the making of yoghurt and labaneh (strained and seasoned yoghurt). We would make sure to buy their dairy products and store them in glass jars to enjoy throughout the season.

The other herb that reminds me of Jericho and grows in fields is molokhia (*Corchorus olitorius*, also called Egyptian spinach or jute mallow). An unusual herb, it has a viscous texture, similar to cooked okra, and there is a whole debate around how viscous it should be. As with every other ingredient in each area in Palestine—and sometimes in each family—people prepare it differently. We make a stew with it that has either meat or chicken and always garlic and fresh coriander. Some people add a tomato to reduce the viscosity, while others boil it for longer to increase the viscosity. Some prefer to finely chop molokhia, while others use the whole leaves. In Jericho markets there are usually heaps of molokhia branches for sale as people dry it for winter and enjoy it at any time of the year.

Jericho is an arid area in the middle of the desert, and yet it's lush in blooming greenery. In Jericho, fields are filled with growing green leaves, such as khobeizeh (*Althaea officinalis* or marshmallow), to be sautéed with onions, olive oil, and sumac. Sumac is often used with sautéed herbs as it adds a tangy, tart flavour. Silek (chard) is also found in these fields.

The fields are watered with groundwater from springs. One of them is called Ein ad Duyuk. It has a pool, and we would sometimes go there for a swim, and later, a barbecue with dishes made from produce from Jericho's fields prepared by my grandmother or her friends. Al-Auja is another spring in the north of Jericho, an impressive place, with waterfalls running down the mountain. We would often go there to admire those waterfalls in the middle of the desert, and much later, when filming *Teta's Kitchen*, I spent time with the Bedouin community that live in the area, where we cooked a fabulous mansaf.

Historically, the agriculture around Jericho centered around date tree farms, which produce the best dates. The area is also known for small, flavorful bananas known as *abu namla*, which translates to "the father of the ant" because they have black speckles on the yellow skin.

It has been sad going back to visit this area as the Bedouin population has been forced out by the Israeli occupation and cloistered into limited fields. The water is being diverted to Israeli settlements in the area.

The tangible impact of colonialism on that part of the West Bank is visible in the effects it has had on Palestinian agriculture, access to land and natural sources of water, and restrictions on foraging.

BETHLEHEM

EASTER KNAFEH NESTS

Knafeh, shredded filo dough, is incredibly versatile and comes in all different shapes to produce both sweet and savoury recipes. The dough, sometimes sold as kadaïf or kataifi, traditionally comes from Nablus and is often stuffed with salty Nabulsi cheese. But it's also made in Bethlehem with a twist. There, the vermicelli-like dough is steamed and served with cinnamon, walnuts, pine nuts, and syrup rather than salty cheese. I think the similarity of the thin knafeh dough to the fine twigs of a nest works beautifully for this Easter dessert. This is very simple to make, extremely tasty, and is guaranteed to please chocolate lovers from children to adults.

SYRUP
200 g / 1 cup white sugar
240 ml / 1 cup water
1½ teaspoons fresh lemon juice
A few drops of orange blossom water

NESTS
115 g / ½ cup unsalted butter, melted
250 g / 9 ounces knafeh dough

CHOCOLATE GANACHE
150 g / ⅔ cup heavy cream
150 g / 5¼ ounces 70% dark chocolate

5 small sugar-coated chocolate Easter eggs or fresh rose petals

MAKES 12 NESTS

To make the syrup, in a saucepan, combine the sugar and water over medium heat, stirring until the sugar dissolves and the water boils. Continue to boil until the syrup coats a spoon, about 5 minutes. Stir in the lemon juice and the orange blossom water. Set aside.

Preheat the oven to 180°C / 350°F.

To make the nests, brush some of the melted butter on the inside of each cup of a muffin pan.

In a bowl, combine the knafeh dough and the rest of the butter and mix gently. Try to avoid breaking the knafeh too much. It is also possible to flatten the dough and brush it on both sides with the melted butter. Transfer the dough to the muffin pan, covering the bottoms and sides with a thin layer; it should be about 2½ cm / 1 inch high. Press well on the bottoms so the dough is compacted.

Bake for 12 to 14 minutes, until the dough turns golden. Set aside to cool.

To make the ganache, heat the cream in a saucepan over medium-low heat until hot but not boiling. Break the chocolate into the cream and stir gently with a wooden spoon. Decrease the heat to low and allow the chocolate to melt; it will take a few minutes. The texture will be rough at the beginning, but keep it on the heat and stir until it becomes a smooth, shiny, chocolate ganache. Remove from the stove and leave to cool down.

To assemble the nests, gently flip over the pan to remove the nests. Place them on a tray ready to go into the refrigerator, preferably lined with parchment paper. Drizzle a bit of the syrup on each nest. Fill the centers with the chocolate ganache. Break the small chocolate eggs and sprinkle them on top. You could also sprinkle fresh rose petals over the top as I do sometimes.

SIYAMI-STUFFED GRAPE LEAVES AND COURGETTES

Siyam is the Arabic word for "fasting." The Palestinian year is marked by many days of fasting. Palestinians of Muslim faith fast during daylight hours during the month of Ramadan. Palestinian Christians refrain from eating animal products on Wednesdays and Fridays, depending on their denomination. Lent, the month leading up to Easter, requires fasting of all Christian denominations. Although the cuisine is not religious, it is often adapted to suit religious traditions.

I find it a strong symbol of diversity and brotherhood between Palestinians to see Muslims and Christians gather around a table, preparing the foods used for different religious events.

Stuffed courgettes (zucchini) and rolled grape leaves are delicacies that can be made vegetarian to suit all those fasts. Personally I prefer serving the siyami version of stuffed leaves and courgettes cold or at room temperature and the meat version piping hot.

400 g / 2 cups medium-grain rice, rinsed and drained

2 small onions, finely chopped

5 garlic cloves, finely chopped

½ bunch flat-leaf parsley, leaves only, finely chopped

½ bunch mint leaves, finely chopped

1 small green chilli, finely chopped

1 kg / 2¼ pounds tomatoes

2 teaspoons ground allspice

½ teaspoon ground black pepper

¼ teaspoon ground cardamom

¼ teaspoon ground cumin

¼ teaspoon ground cinnamon

¼ teaspoon ground ginger

¼ teaspoon ground cloves

¼ teaspoon ground nutmeg

In a large bowl, combine the rice, onions, garlic, parsley, mint, and chilli. Finely chop 3 of the tomatoes and add to the rice. Add the allspice, pepper, cardamom, cumin, cinnamon, ginger, cloves, and nutmeg. Finally add 1 tablespoon of salt and 5 tablespoons of olive oil.

Mix well to coat the rice and vegetables with the oil and spices. Set aside.

If the grape leaves are fresh, cut off the hard stalks and blanch the leaves in a large pot of boiling water until tender but firm, about 5 minutes. If the grape leaves are stored in a jar, drain them and rinse under running water to reduce the acidity and saltiness. Set aside a few leaves to line the bottom of the pot.

Slice the remaining tomatoes.

To core the courgettes, cut off the tops, slice lengthwise, and, with a corer or spoon, empty the courgettes until the outside is about 6 mm / ¼ inch thick. (Store the cored insides to use in another recipe, perhaps an omelette with courgettes and zaatar or the recipe for Mafghoussa [page 58]).

Rinse the cored courgettes in a bowl of salted cold water (for 1 liter / 1 quart of water, use 1 tablespoon of fine table salt). Place in a sieve, cored side downwards, to allow the excess water to drain.

Start filling the courgettes with the rice stuffing, but not to the top—leave about 1 cm / ⅜ inch empty as the rice will expand during cooking.

Cover the bottom of a Dutch oven with a dash of olive oil, a few grape leaves, and the sliced tomatoes. Layer the courgettes on top.

Salt
Olive oil
500 g / 18 ounces grape
    leaves (fresh or in a jar
    in brine)
1 kg / 2¼ pounds koussa
    (small Palestinian
    zucchini)
Juice of 2 lemons

SERVES 8

To stuff the rest of the grape leaves, place a leaf flat on your worktop and place approximately 1 teaspoon of the rice stuffing on one side of the leaf. Fold the sides in and roll tightly. Arrange the stuffed grape leaves over the courgettes in the pan.

In a bowl, mix 1 L/ 4¼ cups boiling water, the lemon juice, 1 tablespoon olive oil, and 1 teaspoon salt. Pour the mix in the pot until the water covers the grape leaves. Place a small plate on top to keep the leaves from floating.

Cover the pot with a lid, bring to a boil over high heat, then decrease the heat to medium and leave to simmer for 50 minutes or so. Make sure there is water at the bottom of the pot. If needed, add some boiling water. Steal one stuffed grape leaf and taste to make sure the rice is cooked (unless you intend to be told off at the picnic!). Once everything is cooked, turn off the heat and carefully tilt the pot sideways to drain any leftover water. Replace the lid and leave covered until it has fully cooled down.

To serve, carefully flip over onto a large tray.

MAFGHOUSSA

Mafghoussa means "squashed" in Arabic, and that's because the vegetables are squashed into cold salads once they are roasted. There are different versions of mafghoussa: some are made with tomatoes and laban jameed (salted and dried yoghurt), some are made with olive oil, as I have done here.

The beauty of mafghoussa is that it's a zero-waste recipe. You can use the cored insides of the courgettes (zucchini) or use the entire courgettes; the taste is slightly different, but it's still delicious. I always make mafghoussa when I core courgettes to make Siyami-Stuffed Grape Leaves and Courgettes (page 56).

Mafghoussa is always served cold. This refreshing dish works beautifully with grilled meats on the side or by itself as a meal.

Extra-virgin olive oil
4 garlic cloves, crushed
1 fresh red chilli, thinly
    sliced
500 g / 18 ounces
    courgette interiors (see
    page 56) or chopped
    entire courgettes
1 teaspoon salt
Juice of 1 lemon
30 g / ¼ cup pine nuts
30 g / ½ cup coarsely
    chopped mint and
    parsley leaves
Warm bread, to serve

SERVES 6

In a large frying pan, heat 3 tablespoons of the olive oil over medium-high heat. Add the garlic and sauté until fragrant, about 30 seconds. Add the chilli with its seeds to the garlic and sauté for 2 to 3 minutes, until the garlic and the chilli are softened and lightly coloured. Add the courgette flesh, stir well, decrease the heat to medium, and sauté for 15 to 20 minutes, until well cooked. While you stir, the courgette flesh will slowly break down. Add the salt and the lemon juice and mix well. Transfer the mafghoussa to a bowl and leave it to cool down.

In the meantime, in a small pan, toast the pine nuts in a bit of olive oil over medium heat until lightly coloured and fragrant, about 1 minute. Set aside.

When the mafghoussa has cooled down, sprinkle the mint and parsley and pine nuts on top and drizzle another teaspoon of olive oil on top, then serve with warm bread for scooping.

BAKED AUBERGINES

The best aubergines (eggplants) in Palestine are known to come from the village of Battir to the west of Bethlehem. We use aubergines in all recipes: traditional stuffed aubergine; the Palestinian take on moussaka, baked aubergines; or simply fried aubergine slices to adorn a breakfast table. The sweet softness of baked aubergines is delightful as a vegetarian course or as an accompaniment to grilled meats.

TOMATO SAUCE
Olive oil
1 onion, finely chopped
2 garlic cloves, crushed
½ teaspoon coriander
    seeds
½ teaspoon ground cumin
200 g / 7 ounces ripe
    tomatoes, coarsely
    chopped
2 teaspoons tomato paste
150 ml / ⅔ cup water
Salt and pepper

AUBERGINES
3 large aubergines
    (eggplants)
Olive oil
2 garlic cloves, thinly sliced
½ bunch flat-leaf parsley,
    leaves only, chopped
½ bunch fresh coriander
    (cilantro), chopped
200 g / 7 ounces ripe
    tomatoes, finely diced
Juice of ½ lemon
1 teaspoon dried red
    pepper flakes

SERVES 4

To make the tomato sauce, heat 1 tablespoon olive oil in a large pan over medium-high heat, add the onion, and sauté for 5 minutes. Add the crushed garlic, coriander seeds, cumin, and chopped tomatoes and stir. Add the tomato paste and water. Season to taste with salt and pepper. Decrease the heat to medium and leave to cook for about 25 minutes.

To make the aubergines, preheat the oven to 220°C / 425°F.

Place the aubergines on a baking sheet and roast for about 40 minutes, until completely soft.

In a small pan, heat 1 tablespoon olive oil over medium heat. Add the garlic slivers and fry until they're golden on both sides, about 2 minutes. Set aside.

When the aubergines are done, slice them lengthwise to have two halves. Scoop out the flesh carefully, making sure not to damage the skin, and place in a bowl. Mash the aubergine with a fork. Add the tomato sauce slowly, combining well. Mix in the parsley.

In a separate bowl, combine the coriander and diced tomatoes and mix together.

In another bowl, combine 1 teaspoon olive oil, the lemon juice, and red pepper flakes and mix together.

To assemble the dish, place the aubergine skins on a plate and fill them with the mixture of aubergine flesh and tomato sauce. Top with the diced tomato mixture and red pepper flake garnish. Sprinkle the fried garlic slivers on top. Drizzle with olive oil, if you like, and serve.

S U M M E R

APRICOT
BAKLAWA

200 g / 7 tablespoons
 water
1½ teaspoons ground
 mastic
200 g / 1 cup sugar
500 g / 18 ounces apricots,
 halved and pitted
300 g / 10 ounces unsalted
 butter, melted
500 g / 18 ounces frozen
 filo sheets, thawed
300 g / 10 ounces shelled
 pistachios, crushed in a
 mortar

SYRUP
100 g / 7 tablespoons
 honey
½ teaspoon rose water
Juice of ½ lemon

SERVES 8

Apricots have the shortest peak season of any fruit in Palestine. There are a few weeks of frenzy where we rush to get Mistakawi apricots, said to be the best apricots, from a town next to Bethlehem called Beit Jala. The fruit has that hint of Arabic mastic sweetness and floral notes. As I write this recipe, my mother is cooking batches of apricot jam for the year ahead. People preorder quantities from their farmers. The farmers that have been working for years will just before the season guesstimate quantities they will produce and allocate to each customer a specific quantity. And then we all try to negotiate here and there.

   The best way to eat these apricots is as is—just give them a light wash. I like them very cold, so I put them in a bowl with some ice cubes. This recipe makes a beautifully fragrant, slightly sweet dessert.

In a medium-size pot, combine the water, mastic, and 100 g / ½ cup of the sugar and bring to a boil. Decrease the heat to a simmer, add the apricots, and poach for 10 minutes, until they're tender but not squishy. Drain the apricots, reserving the cooking liquid.

Put half the drained apricots into a bowl and mash them until they have the consistency of a compote. Reserve the remaining apricots.

To assemble the baklawa, brush a 24 by 36 cm / 9 by 13-inch baking pan with butter and line it with parchment paper. Butter the parchment paper, too.

It's very important to keep the filo sheets moist as you work with them. The best way to do so is to keep them covered with plastic wrap, then a wet cloth on top. Make sure the wet cloth doesn't touch the filo sheets. Take the filo sheets, one at a time, and brush one side with butter and put it in the pan. Stack 8 buttered filo sheets, then spread a bit of the apricot mix and sprinkle with some of the pistachios. Repeat the process and arrange the remaining apricots and pistachios on top of the filo. Finish with a final layer of three buttered filo sheets. With a sharp knife, slice the baklawa diagonally in two directions to create diamond shapes.

Preheat the oven to 180°C / 350°F.

Bake the baklawa for about 40 minutes, until golden and crisp. Cool on a rack.

To make the syrup, mix the honey, the remaining 100 g / ½ cup sugar, the reserved apricot cooking liquid, and the rose water in a saucepan. Bring to a boil over medium-high heat. Decrease the heat and simmer for 5 minutes, until the syrup coats a dipped spoon. Add the lemon juice, give it a stir, take it off the heat, and allow it to cool.

An hour before serving, drizzle the syrup all over the baklawa to allow the flavors to mix together.

SUNDAY AFTERNOONS WITH SIDO MICHEL

Sunday afternoons growing up were full of tasty meals cooked by my maternal grandmother, Teta Julia, followed by seasonal fresh fruit. In Palestine, the fruit can range from prickly pears with their neon flesh to giant juicy oranges to football-size watermelons.

After the meal it was then the habit of my grandfather, Sido Michel, to pull out his sun chair and sit on the balcony at the back of his house overlooking the well-tended garden and read. From an early age, as his oldest grandchild, I was invited to join him, browsing through French magazines or newspapers or sometimes one of my grandmother's cookbooks. Then my grandfather would tell me stories of his life.

Sido Michel grew up in France and trained as a doctor in Beirut before coming back to Bethlehem, his ancestral home, to practise. He worked in medical centres and clinics across our city, in its refugee camps and surrounding villages, as well as in neighbouring Jerusalem. For many years, he was director of the Holy Family Hospital, then a general hospital. Later he established a clinic and worked as a consultant with patients coming to see him from all over Palestine. Very often they would bring him gifts of food. I remember sampling with him the finest crunchy apples from the southern West Bank; halawa (elsewhere known as halva), the sweet tahinia-based treat from Nablus; golden baladi (local) honey; and creamy laban jameed from local Bedouin families.

There is no doubt that my grandfather loved Palestinian cuisine. He treated every dish made by my grandmother as a celebration, but he also retained a soft spot for the flavours of his childhood in Paris. He poured into me his food memories and, of course, in time I learned like him to savour the joys of a warm, fluffy croissant and a packed charcuterie board. Sometimes we would take family holidays in France together, where he would introduce me to the dishes closest to his heart. I would delight in these mouthwatering adventures, and when we were back home I would start planning our next trip and what and where we would eat. Sometimes the results could be quite unexpected.

On one vacation by the sea, my parents, grandparents, and a few family friends gathered in a restaurant for lunch. I was about ten years old at the time, as was another child who was seated with me at the end of the table. As the adults chatted away, nobody paid attention to our orders. Imagine their surprise when we were served the largest platter of *fruits de mer* (seafood). Determined to show we were up to the challenge, we happily spent the afternoon munching through a pile of oysters, clams, mussels, lobster, and langoustines. My grandfather loved to recount this story and laugh at how daring my palate could be.

Another favourite family tale dates back to when I was about six years old. My glands had become worryingly swollen, and I was sent to a specialist for examination, though even that doctor was at a loss to explain it. At his clinic, my grandfather asked if I had been tested for toxoplasmosis, only for the doctor to respond that this was unlikely as I had not been close to cats and that I was too young to be eating raw meat, the two main sources of this parasitic infection. Chuckling, my grandfather requested the toxoplasmosis test which, of course, turned out to be positive. This stunned the specialist until my grandfather revealed to him that at this tender age, I had already been demanding steak tartare.

Sometimes Sido would lead me down the path of overindulgence. On one wonderful occasion, the two of us went off shopping in Paris, claiming we were just planning to buy a couple of goodies. Instead we returned from the charcuterie with every local delicacy imaginable, from *tête de veau* (calf's head) to thick slices of *jambon* (ham) and rich, buttery foie gras. It is his legacy that has also left me with passions for bread and cheese—two staples that combine the beauty of his Palestinian and French identities.

Sido would always be outraged if any meal was served without bread on the table, even if the main course was a carbohydrate, such as pasta or rice. Cheese was another must. Whenever one of us travelled to France, we delighted in returning with a selection of French cheeses to share. In Palestine, the day-to-day cheese offerings were more limited to the supermarket's Gouda or a salty Nabulsi, but this would not hold us back. From Sido Michel, I have acquired the habit of eating cheese as a midnight snack. If I wake up in the middle of the night, I naturally head to the fridge. My grandmother would often wake to find the contents of her dairy drawer had been devoured.

While he may have been a great bon vivant, Sido was above all a people person. He always made it clear to me that being a doctor involved not only treating patients' physical complaints, but also listening to them and learning their habits. He was a truly gentle man who became expert at recognising the similarities in all of us.

Many of the patients became his friends, and he liked to visit them. Sometimes on those Sunday afternoons, before our reading sessions, Sido would take Teta Julia and I on such an excursion, and food would always feature. We might go to see farmers in their citrus groves in Jericho, stop off at the honey farms of Al-Ubeidiya, or visit the grape molasses shops in Halhul or al-Khader.

My grandfather continued working in his clinic until the afternoon before he died. Now, many years after his passing, I still meet people who remember him, his small kindnesses, and his dedication to the community. Some of his former patients recall his love of local products, too. All in all, Sido Michel set an impressive example that I try to emulate at the same time that I try to keep our rituals. I love to read on a Sunday afternoon, and I have to admit that I've never given up the habit of midnight raids on the fridge.

KA'EK
AL-QUDS
AND EGGS

400 g / 3⅓ cups all-
  purpose flour, plus
  more for the work
  surface
60 g / ¼ cup powdered
  whole milk
1 teaspoon salt
1 tablespoon baking soda
1 teaspoon instant yeast
2 tablespoons extra-virgin
  olive oil, plus more for
  shaping
120 ml / ½ cup warm
  water
3 tablespoons water
1 egg white
40 g / 4½ tablespoons
  toasted sesame seeds
8 eggs
1 tablespoon zaatar spice
  blend

SERVES 4

A morning visit to Jerusalem is never complete without a newspaper, a ka'ek, two oven-baked eggs, and a small bunched-up paper filled with zaatar.

The sesame seed–coated bread is baked fresh in wood-fired ovens in bakeries across Palestine every morning, then transported on small wooden carts across the streets. Vendors call out "ka'ek, ka'ek" with a musical variety of intonations.

An ideal sandwich bread, ka'ek tastes best with the oven-baked eggs and a pinch of extra-salty zaatar. It is also delicious with falafel (page 220), labaneh (strained and seasoned yoghurt), Nabulsi cheese, or anything else that crosses your mind or inspires your palate.

To make the ka'eks, in a large bowl, whisk together the flour, powdered milk, salt, baking soda, and yeast. Make a well in the middle and add 1 tablespoon of the olive oil and the warm water. Mix well by hand until you have a homogenous dough. Transfer the dough to a floured work surface and knead the dough for 10 minutes. Cover with a cloth and leave in a warm place for 1 hour.

Flour the work surface, place the dough on the surface, and cut into four pieces.

Line a baking sheet with parchment paper. With oiled hands, working with one piece of dough at a time, form the dough into a ring. Slowly stretch it into the oblong shape of the Jerusalem ka'ek. Place the ka'ek on the prepared baking sheet. Repeat with the remaining pieces of dough. Cover the ka'eks with a cloth and leave to rise for 15 minutes.

Preheat the oven to 200°C / 400°F.

Whisk 2 tablespoons of the water and egg white together and brush over the tops of the dough. Mix the sesame seeds with the remaining 1 tablespoon water, and sprinkle evenly onto the ka'ek.

Bake for 25 minutes, or until the breads are golden. You may have to rotate the baking sheet to get an even colour.

Once the breads are baked, decrease the oven temperature to 180°C / 350°F.

To make the eggs, place them in a muffin pan, one whole egg per cavity. Bake for 30 minutes.

To serve, slice each ka'ek open as for a sandwich. Peel the eggs, mash them with a fork in a bowl, add the zaatar and remaining 1 tablespoon olive oil, and mix to combine. Stuff the ka'eks with the egg mixture and enjoy!

BETHLEHEM

MANAKISH WITH FRESH AND DRIED TOMATOES, PARSLEY CREAM, AND OLIVE OIL

Manakish are fluffy, crispy flatbreads that you see in every bakery around Palestine and neighbouring countries. Traditionally topped with zaatar spice mix, they can be made with a multitude of toppings for breakfast or a snack.

The best manakish are the ones baked fresh in a wood-burning oven, with the toppings ranging from baladi white cheese to mincemeat, taken hot in a paper wrap, and enjoyed while gazing at the hubbub of the souk.

To make the dough, in a small bowl, dissolve the yeast in the warm water. Leave for 4 to 5 minutes, until it starts to bubble.

In a large bowl, mix the flour, sugar, and yeast mixture. Cover and leave for 15 minutes. Mix in 5 teaspoons of the olive oil and the salt.

Flour a work surface. Turn the dough onto the floured surface and knead the dough with your hands for 5 minutes until homogenous. Cover with a cloth and allow to rise in a warm place for 30 minutes.

Preheat the oven to 180°C / 350°F. Line a baking sheet with parchment paper.

On a floured surface, divide the dough into four pieces. Flatten each piece into a round circle using either a rolling pin or your fingertips. Mix the sumac and the remaining ½ teaspoon olive oil, and brush onto the top of the breads. Place the flatbreads on the prepared baking sheet.

Place the sheet on the bottom rack of the oven and bake for about 15 minutes, until the dough is golden.

To prepare the toppings, drain the oil from the sun-dried tomatoes, reserving the oil. Coarsely chop the dried tomatoes.

In a bowl, mix the parsley with the crème fraiche and the salt.

Spread the parsley cream over the baked manakish and top with the thinly sliced tomatoes and the chopped dried tomatoes. Drizzle the reserved oil over the tops.

DOUGH
1½ teaspoons dry baking yeast
120 ml / ½ cup warm water
130 g / 1 cup plus 1 tablespoon all-purpose flour, plus more for the work surface
1½ teaspoons sugar
5½ teaspoons extra-virgin olive oil
½ teaspoon salt
1 teaspoon ground sumac

TOPPINGS
8 sun-dried tomatoes in oil
½ bunch flat-leaf parsley, leaves only, finely chopped
3 tablespoons crème fraîche
½ teaspoon salt
2 fresh tomatoes, thinly sliced

SERVES 4

GREEN SHATTA

Of all the condiments that complement the flavours of Palestinian cuisine, the spicy shattas (hot sauces) are my favourites. Traditionally we make a red shatta with fermented red chillies.

This green shatta recipe keeps the zing of the fresh chillies and the citrusy pepperiness of the fresh coriander (cilantro). It's ideal for complementing a labaneh plate or garnishing a lentil soup.

250 g / 9 ounces green chillies, stemmed and coarsely chopped
1 garlic clove, coarsely chopped
½ teaspoon salt
80 g / 2¾ ounces fresh coriander (cilantro), stems removed and leaves coarsely chopped
1 tablespoon fresh lemon juice
1 tablespoon extra-virgin olive oil

MAKES 250 G / 1 CUP

In a food processor, combine the chillies, garlic, and salt. Process into a chunky texture. Add the coriander leaves, lemon juice, and olive oil. Process into a fine yet grainy texture. Store in an airtight jar in the refrigerator for up to a week.

BETHLEHEM

LABANEH BALLS WITH NIGELLA SEEDS

Essential to Palestinian breakfasts is labaneh (strained and seasoned yoghurt). There are many different kinds of labaneh but only two ways to enjoy it. Either you have it in its fresh form, which is acidic, creamy, rich, and fluffy, or you have it dried into balls. These balls are usually plain, but they can also be served coated with green zaatar or purple-red ground sumac or other spices. At Akub I serve them rolled in sumac, zaatar, and a mix of turmeric and crushed Aleppo pepper.

Some people add spices to the labaneh balls and serve them immediately or store them in olive oil. Others store them plain and add the spices at serving time. In both cases, place the balls in a glass jar, cover them with olive oil, and store at room temperature in the dark for up to 3 months.

I personally prefer making them plain and coating them with spices or nigella seeds just before serving.

1 kg / 4 cups Greek yoghurt or goat milk yoghurt
1 teaspoon salt
2 tablespoons nigella seeds
1 tablespoon extra-virgin olive oil

MAKES 25 LABANEH BALLS

Line a sieve with cheesecloth. Add the yoghurt and the salt and mix well. Tie the cheesecloth very tightly around the yoghurt over the sieve, put the sieve in a bowl, and refrigerate for 2 days until the liquid whey drains out.

Check the labaneh; it may need to be tied tighter and left for up to another 12 hours in the refrigerator to get firm.

To make the balls, spread a dry a cheesecloth on a baking sheet. Remove 15 to 20 grams or a spoonful of labaneh and roll it by hand into a small ball and place on the prepared tray. Repeat until all the labaneh has been rolled into balls. Cover the balls with another cloth and refrigerate for a day to firm up.

Place the nigella seeds in a bowl and toss the labaneh balls in the seeds until they are coated on all sides. Serve on a plate with the olive oil drizzled on top.

FIG SALAD

8 figs
2 tablespoons extra-virgin
    olive oil
1 teaspoon ground sumac

SERVES 4

This fig salad is actually the simplest recipe in the book, and yet it might be the one with the most complex flavours as these are given to us by nature without intervention from cooks. Figs are a magical fruit that have a very deep, intense flavour that is both sweet and at the same time extremely close to savoury.

This recipe combines the three flavors of Palestine: figs, olive oil, and sumac. There are two fig seasons in Palestine, the first one at the beginning of summer, when we get the large green Daafur figs, and the second in midsummer, when the small green and purple figs ripen. This recipe works with both of them.

Cut the figs from the top down all four sides but not all the way through, to keep the four pieces attached at the bottom. Drizzle the olive oil and sprinkle the sumac on top and serve.

DEAD SEA SALT

Drive just outside Bethlehem and the verdant green of our olive groves and gardens gives way to a dramatically different rocky desert landscape. Forty-five minutes away, with your ears popping from the steep decline, you arrive at the Dead Sea, the lowest point on earth. This was once an impressive place, famous for its minerals and its buoyancy, which has produced so many quirky photographs of visitors floating while reading newspapers and the like. But today, the waters, along with those of the River Jordan that feeds into it, are sadly diminished.

Even though a large portion of the Dead Sea lies within the occupied West Bank, few places along the water's edge are accessible to Palestinians. The retreating shoreline is dotted with Israeli settlement resorts and companies extracting minerals. There is only one Palestinian salt producer still located there: the West Bank Salt Company. Abu Hussein has been at the site since before the 1967 war. With steely determination, Abu Hussein and his son, general manager Hussam Hallaq, have remained there.

The first time I ever headed off the main road toward the company, I stopped by the remains of an abandoned hotel. It looked strangely familiar, and I soon realised that this eerie spot was the Lido Hotel, which I had seen in my grandparents' holiday photographs. A few decades ago, when they visited, the sea was a few steps away. Now its ruins are 2 to 3 kilometres (1¼ to 2 miles) from the shoreline.

Hussam nodded knowingly when I told him this. His family's story is dominated by the struggle to access the salty waters. For me, the company epitomises the prized quality of Palestinian resilience, or *sumud*. There have been many attempts to expel the Hallaqs from the land and to close their factory, and they still face challenges. Yet with strength of will, they remain there, extracting what for me is the highest quality of sea salt in the world, with a taste that goes back millennia.

During a tour, Hussam showed me all the types of high-quality salts his company refines with natural methods. However, I got fixated on the mound of grey material that constantly lay just behind him, tantalisingly out of reach. "Hussam, what is that?" I finally asked. He explained that it was the salt extracted from the sea before the cleaning process. Of course, that was the raw material that I then craved for my kitchen. That day, I returned home with my car loaded down with a 20-kilogram (44-pound) bag of that unrefined salt. Hussam had helped me load it into the car, shaking his head and asking, "Are you really going to use that?"

Now, a few years later, Hussam continues to pack that unrefined salt for me. It is what we use in Bethlehem at Fawda restaurant and at Akub, my restaurant in London. I delight in bringing international chefs to the West Bank Salt Company and loading them up with raw salt to take back. It has a very distinctive taste: it's not briny but sharp, pure, unpolluted salt. It is a salt that has had little exposure to living beings because the Dead Sea's extreme salinity means that no creatures can survive in it.

As anyone visiting Hussam easily sees, there is a shocking environmental disaster unfolding at the Dead Sea, and it is happening at an alarming pace. This idyllic place, so treasured in historical and religious literature, is vanishing for future generations. The River Jordan, which flows from the Golan Heights in the very north and through the Sea of Galilee, no longer brings abundant waters to replenish the Dead Sea. The river's flow is supposed to be split between Jordan, Syria, and Israel but has suffered greatly from over-extraction and pollution and is now little more than an unhealthy, muddy trickle. The Dead Sea has been dropping at a rate of over a metre (3 feet) a year, and various international efforts to try to reverse the trend have come to nought.

To some extent, the magical properties of the Dead Sea itself are leading to its destruction. Potash—used mostly for fertilizer—is a valuable commodity and a longtime reason for water removal. Then there are the beauty products and spas, which have their origins as far back as Cleopatra. She could never have imagined the mass tourism of today with its ongoing negative ecological impact.

It always impresses me how at the West Bank Salt Company, very small amounts of water are lost. Only salt crystals stay in the drying ponds while the water gets pumped back to the sea. There is a tube that now stretches for 2 kilometres (1¼ miles) down to the water's edge and then a second tube that returns the water to the sea. The salt is processed, washed, and cleaned on site.

This is how the factory has functioned since before 1967. Methods of production have not changed. Indeed, they cannot be changed. The site lies in what is known as Area C of the West Bank—the 60 percent that falls under Israel's full control. It is virtually impossible for Palestinians to get Israeli planning permission to erect new structures here and so only those that existed before 1967 can be used for salt production by Hussam's team. This is why the packing process takes place in Jericho.

Despite all the challenges, the company supplies the tastiest salt imaginable.

LOUKMET MOLOKHIA

3 tablespoons extra-virgin olive oil

5 garlic cloves, half crushed and half thinly sliced

½ teaspoon coriander seeds

½ teaspoon ground allspice

1 teaspoon salt

1 bunch fresh coriander (cilantro) leaves, finely chopped and stems discarded

75 g / 3 cups fresh molokhia leaves, or 1 to 1½ cups frozen, finely chopped (set a few fresh whole leaves aside for garnish)

Juice of 1 lemon

475 ml / 2 cups water

200 g / 1 cup medium-grain rice

4 small green chillies, stemmed and halved lengthwise

1 lemon, unwaxed, sliced

SERVES 6

Loukmeh in Arabic means "mouthful." This dish is an interpretation of the traditional way molokhia (*Corchorus olitorius*; also called Egyptian spinach or jute mallow) is usually prepared. This green is usually cooked in the summer with fresh leaves. It is found in Palestine, Lebanon, Egypt, Tunisia, and Japan. In Palestine, the best molokhia is grown in Jericho.

Molokhia is an acquired taste, but it was one of my favorite dishes as a child and still is. It is disappearing in its winter form, thanks to the availability of refrigeration, fewer people are drying it. Both forms of molokhia—fresh and dried—have very distinct and different tastes. In this recipe, fresh or frozen can be used to make this small vegetarian mouthful to be served in a spoon almost as an amuse-bouche.

In a pot, heat 1 tablespoon of the olive oil over medium-high heat. Add the crushed garlic, coriander seeds, allspice, ½ teaspoon of the salt, and half the chopped coriander leaves, and stir. Add the chopped molokhia leaves and stir. When the molokhia wilts, add water to cover it. Reduce the heat to medium and cook for 10 to 12 minutes, uncovered, until the molokhia is tender. Stir in the lemon juice.

Meanwhile, bring the 475 ml / 2 cups water and the remaining ½ teaspoon salt to a boil over medium heat. Stir in the rice, cover the pot, reduce the heat to low, and leave it to cook for 15 to 20 minutes; do not allow the pot to go dry until the rice is cooked. Keep the pot covered and leave it to rest so that it absorbs the steam, then fluff the rice with a fork.

In a small pan, heat another 1 tablespoon of the olive oil over medium-high heat and fry the chillies on both sides until they are cooked and the skins are slightly charred. Set the chillies aside on paper towels.

In the same pan, fry the thinly sliced garlic cloves over medium heat until golden and crispy, about 3 minutes. Set aside on paper towels.

Add the remaining 1 tablespoon of olive oil to the same pan, fry the remaining chopped coriander until crisp, and drain on paper towels.

In the same frying pan, fry the fresh whole molokhia leaves until crispy, about 15 minutes, and drain on paper towels.

To assemble the dish, scoop up a rounded ball of rice with a serving spoon and push with your fingers in the middle of the ball to create a hollow. Fill it with molokhia, then cover with some more rice to end up with a round ball of rice with the molokhia in the heart.

Place a large spoonful of the molokhia stew in a bowl, then set the rice ball on it. Sprinkle with the fried coriander, chillies, garlic, fried molokhia leaves, and a fresh lemon slice. Continue to assemble bowls until all the ingredients are used. And all of that is a couple of mouthfuls of molokhia pleasure.

BETHLEHEM

BARBECUED TOMATO SALAD

On a Palestinian barbecue, of course, there are the classics: kebabs, lamb chops, pork chops, chicken, and marinated chicken skewers. But we also grill whole small onions, tomatoes, and chilli peppers. The heat from a barbecue is fantastic if you manage it correctly. Start off with things like sujuk sausages (spicy, dry fermented sausages), then move to chicken, lamb, and vegetables. This tomato salad is easy and delicious, the ideal accompaniment to whatever you have on the barbecue.

700 g / 1½ pounds ripe tomatoes
2 tablespoons extra-virgin olive oil
1½ teaspoons dried zaatar leaves, chopped
½ teaspoon coarse sea salt
2 tablespoons fresh spearmint leaves, chopped
1 tablespoon peppermint leaves, chopped
Juice of 1 lemon
1 tablespoon crumbled laban jameed (see page 33)

SERVES 6

Prepare a gas or charcoal fire in the barbecue to be flaming hot.

In a bowl, toss the tomatoes with the olive oil, zaatar leaves, and salt. Place the tomatoes directly on the barbecue grill. Reserve the oil remaining in the bowl.

Turn the tomatoes on the grill, until they are nicely charred on all sides; this should take about 3 minutes. Move the tomatoes to the higher shelf of the barbecue or to the side of the barbecue away from the direct heat if a shelf isn't available. Cook for another 2 to 3 minutes, until cooked through without charring more. Remove from the heat.

Add both types of mint to the flavored oil that remains in the bowl. Add the lemon juice and mix well.

Cut the cooked tomatoes into quarters with a very sharp knife so they're not damaged or squashed and transfer to a serving dish. Drizzle the herbed oil on top. Sprinkle the laban jameed on top to finish.

AUBERGINES ROASTED WITH TAHINIA

We use aubergine (eggplant) in all manner of recipes. It is a wonderful vegetable when it's roasted, charred, and smoky, and we all know how fantastic baba ghanouj is. This recipe works as a starter or as part of a shared table and it screams summer to my palate.

Preheat the oven to 200°C / 400°F.

Rub the aubergines with the olive oil and place them in a roasting pan. Roast for about 45 minutes, turning them every 10 minutes so they cook evenly.

Meanwhile, prepare the tahinia sauce. Combine the tahinia, 2½ tablespoons of the olive oil, 2 of the garlic cloves, the lemon juice, chillies, and salt in a food processor. With the motor running, add the water slowly and continue mixing until the sauce is smooth.

Place the aubergines on a serving dish, and press down so the skin cracks. Drizzle on the tahinia sauce, and sprinkle the dill, parsley, nigella seeds and coriander seeds on top. Then sprinkle on the pomegranate seeds and the pine nuts.

Thinly slice the remaining 2 garlic cloves. Heat a little oil in a small pan over medium heat. Add the garlic and fry until golden, 2 minutes. Drizzle the oil with the garlic on top, and serve.

4 large aubergines
Olive oil
95 g / ⅓ cup tahinia
4 garlic cloves
Juice of 2 lemons
2 chillies, finely chopped
½ tsp fine salt
6 tablespoons water
1 bunch dill, fronds
    coarsely chopped and
    stems discarded
1 bunch flat-leaf parsley,
    leaves only, coarsely
    chopped
1 teaspoon nigella seeds
1 teaspoon coriander seeds
2 tablespoons
    pomegranate seeds
2 tablespoons toasted
    pine nuts

SERVES 4

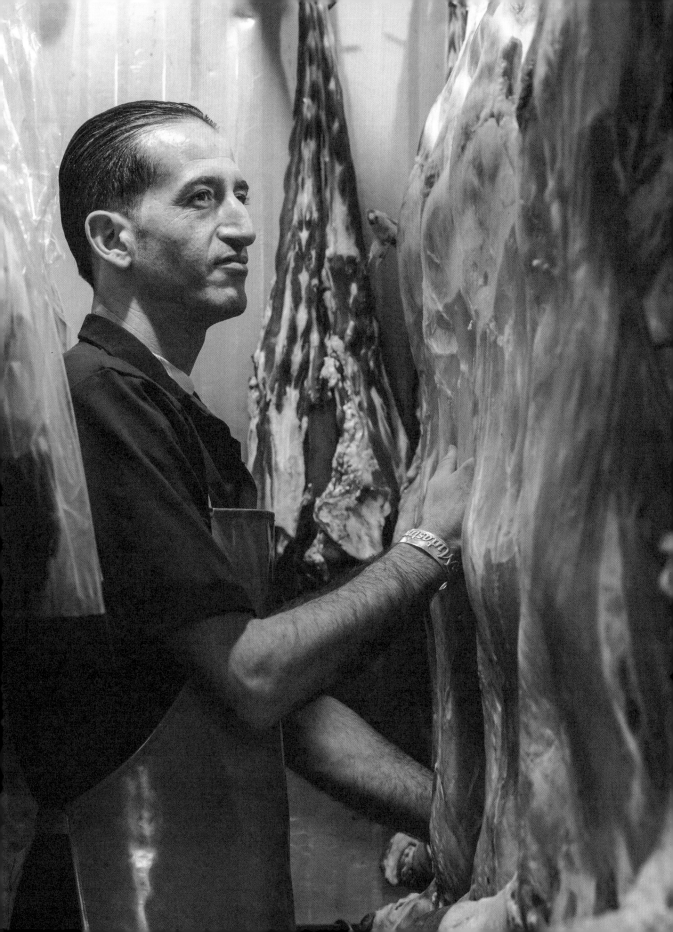

KIBBEH NAYYEH

250 g / 1½ cups fine-grain bulgur wheat
½ kg / 1 pound lamb or goat mince (ground lamb or goat)
½ onion, finely chopped
1 teaspoon salt
½ teaspoon allspice
¼ teaspoon ground black pepper
¼ teaspoon dried red pepper flakes
¼ teaspoon ground cumin
¼ teaspoon ground cardamom
1 tablespoon extra-virgin olive oil
Juice of ½ lemon

SERVES 6

Kibbeh is a classic dish made of ground meat, spices, and bulgur wheat, shaped into a ball.

Kibbeh nayyeh, or raw kibbeh, is commonly shared across the region and especially in the northern areas of Palestine. I have enjoyed the taste of raw meat since I was young, but I know it is not for everyone. Kibbeh nayyeh is the perfect middle ground for anybody who's not a fan of a tartare. Even though I personally love tartare, the texture of the kibbeh nayyeh is milder and softer, while the spices and bulgur give a delicate fragrance to the meat.

In a bowl, pour water over the bulgur wheat, making sure it's covered with 1 cm / ⅜ inch of water above its surface. Set aside for 1 hour; if the bulgur absorbs all the water, add some more. When the bulgur is soft, drain it through a sieve. Use your hands to squeeze out all the water.

Use a mortar and pestle to pound the meat, one-third at a time, to a thin texture, until you can cut into it with a spoon. As you finish each batch, transfer to a large bowl. Add the onion, salt, and spices to the meat, and mix together.

Divide the mixture into two to four batches. Pound each batch in the mortar and pestle until it is all of a consistent texture. This must be done quickly, so the heat of the mortar and pestle doesn't alter the consistency or the colour of the meat.

Combine all the batches in a bowl. Add ½ teaspoon of the olive oil and the lemon juice. Mix quickly so the acidity of the lemon juice doesn't cook the meat.

Spread the meat on a plate. Drizzle the remaining 2½ teaspoons of olive oil on top. Use a fork to add some patterns, then serve.

THE NATSHEH BROTHERS

At the heart of first-class cuisine is top-quality meat and produce. I am so fortunate to live close to the original shop of the best butchers in Bethlehem, in the heart of the crowded old souk.

A visit to one of the two Natsheh Butcheries is not for the weak-hearted. There are no neatly packaged, precisely weighed cuts as found in a supermarket. Instead, there are fresh carcasses of sheep, goats, and cows hanging just inside the entrance of the constantly busy store and filling the deep fridge inside. While their discerning customers sit and wait, sipping the complimentary Arabic coffee, the men of the Natsheh family skillfully chop the desired cuts of meat to order. There is constant chatter as the butchers and the shoppers exchange tips on how best to prepare and serve different Palestinian dishes in which meat traditionally takes a role. After school or during holidays, the boys of the Natsheh family also form part of the shop team, lending a hand and learning the business.

The Natsheh butchers carry the pride that comes from working for generations in the same trade. They own their own livestock farms, keeping sheep and goats, which brings an extra level of commitment and expertise. As a commemorative stone close to the shops testifies, the souk was opened in 1929, during the British Mandate period. The marketplace was designed by a Bethlehem architect, Elias Anastas. One of its original purposes was to impose regulations on butchers as in the past locals ran their own makeshift operations on their farms or outside their homes. The majority of professional butcher stores have remained in the original, main square of the souk ever since it was established.

Over the years, the Natsheh business has become part of our town's daily life and family traditions. As a young child, I was rarely taken to the souk, but I grew up hearing constant references to the butchers. After becoming a customer and working with them for years, I still find wonderful new connections. Once, when my father persuaded me to recreate his aunt's braciole recipe, my description of how to cut the meat thinly so that I could pound it and make it into a roulade drew a smile from the old uncle of the young butcher I had ordered it from. He remembered my great-aunt asking for just the same thing.

Lamb meat, or mutton, is the main type of meat used in Palestinian cuisine. Our local variety of sheep, known as Awassi, is common to the wider region. It has a distinct, relatively mild flavour, with the fat, called *liyeh*, concentrated in a pouch under its flat tail. The basics that butchers must master include how to grind lamb meat for kebabs, adding parsley, finely chopped onions, and sometimes green chillies; how to cut meat for cutlets; and how to prepare a whole animal. For special occasions, whole sheep are often sent off to be slow-cooked in the local, communal wood-burning oven. Mansaf is such a popular dish that you will often find customers ordering large lamb cuts to be boiled and added to the top of a steaming tray of rice with lashings of laban jameed.

In Western cooking, nose-to-tail eating has become a modern trend to tackle food waste and show respect for the life of the animals we use to feed us. However, it is worth noting that in some parts of the world, including Palestine, this idea has always been the norm. At the Natsheh butchers, you see how this works in practice. It is not just the prized cuts that are on display but also the delicious, nutrient-rich organs, the tails, and the feet. When shopping for meat, the weight of the order often includes the bones. These can be cleaned and taken home as most people continue to make meat stocks at home, adding herbs, onions, and vegetables. Fat is stored for use in shawarma skewers, layered between the meat for moisture and taste.

I always value my conversations with the Natsheh butchers and admire their professionalism. It is a great privilege to be allowed to walk into their fridge to select a piece of meat or the entire sheep that I would like to buy for my restaurant. The butchers are also ready to indulge some of my experiments. It is uncommon to age beef in Palestine, and I know the Natshehs were not particularly convinced when I first asked them to do it for me, but they were ready to try, and soon I had converted them to the idea. They even began calling me to give updates and suggest that they keep the meat longer. This meant that we eventually came to dry-age beef for 6 weeks. Several years on from our first aged *côte de boeuf*, I know that today, the Natshehs only take home aged beef for their own kitchens.

The butchers maintain high standards through the whole process of feeding, breeding, and slaughtering their animals. Small businesses like theirs ensure a more sustainable, ethical kind of farming with a high standard of animal welfare. In the hectic marketplace, the Natshehs also impose careful health and hygiene measures and keep the perfect temperature controls. I am so confident in their practices that I often bring visitors for a stop at the store when I do food tours in Bethlehem. I enjoy taking a fresh lamb's liver from the butchers, slicing it, and adding a dash of olive oil, a little salt, and a squeeze of lemon before feeding it to my surprised guests.

KOFTA IN GRAPE LEAVES

These round beef meatballs tightly wrapped in grape leaves are maybe one of my favorite recipes from my mother's repertoire. I try to replicate it and use it as an inspiration for new dishes, variations on the theme. Notably in Akub restaurant in London, we've replaced the meat with skate; at Fawda in Bethlehem we use cheeses. Here I'm sharing the original recipe, which says home to me.

To prepare the grape leaves, first remove the stems. Blanch the leaves in a large pot of boiling water for 2 to 3 minutes, until tender. Drain well.

Mix the meat with the onion, salt, allspice, nutmeg, cardamom, black pepper, cinnamon, and parsley. Divide the meat into twelve portions.

Preheat the oven to 180°C / 350°F.

Wrap each portion of meat in grape leaves to make balls, using about two leaves per meatball.

Arrange the tomatoes and wrapped meatballs in a baking pan, drizzle with the olive oil, and sprinkle a bit of salt on top. Bake for 30 minutes. *Sahtain*!

24 to 26 small grape leaves
500 g / 18 ounces beef mince (ground beef)
1 onion, finely chopped
2 teaspoons salt, plus more for sprinkling
1 teaspoon ground allspice
¼ teaspoon ground nutmeg
¼ teaspoon ground cardamom
¼ teaspoon ground black pepper
¼ teaspoon ground cinnamon
1 bunch flat-leaf parsley, leaves only, finely chopped
5 tomatoes, sliced
2 tablespoons extra-virgin olive oil

SERVES 4

ROSTO MARIAM

3 tablespoons samneh
    (ghee)
1 kg / 2¼ pounds beef
    chuck, cut into 3 cm /
    1¼-inch cubes
5 garlic cloves, crushed
1 teaspoon salt
½ teaspoon ground black
    pepper
½ teaspoon ground
    allspice
¼ teaspoon ground
    nutmeg
¼ teaspoon ground
    cinnamon
2 tablespoons white
    vinegar
600 ml / 1½ to 2½ cups
    water

SERVES 4 TO 6

Mariam was my great-grandmother, another much loved and talked-about relative whom I unfortunately never got to meet. But her recipe was passed down to me and became an essential beef stew and a family tradition.

It is a stew, even though we call it Mariam's roast. Any of Mariam's great-grandchildren, my cousins and I, would recognise the scent of Rosto Mariam wherever we are in the world.

Apparently, Mariam was a fantastic cook, and she did her own variations on traditional dishes as well as cooking Palestinian classics in her kitchen.

For this recipe, she replaced wine with vinegar. I can imagine how, in her home, in the outskirts of Bethlehem where they had large gardens full of almonds, figs, apricots, walnuts, and grapes, this vinegar was most likely made by her. She would serve the stew accompanied with whatever vegetable was in season on the side, or sometimes as is.

There was a cheerful little stream of water that ran across the rich soil of my great-grandparents' land. As a kid, I remember joyously going to that stone home and picking apricots, almonds, and walnuts that tasted different than anywhere else.

Each generation and member in the family had the recipe passed down to them and probably added little variations. One of the secrets of Mariam's cooking was the unlimited use of samneh (ghee/clarified butter).

In a large pot over medium-high heat, melt the samneh. Add the beef cubes, garlic, salt, and pepper. Cook the meat cubes for about 10 minutes, stirring until they are evenly cooked on all sides. Add the allspice, nutmeg, cinnamon, and vinegar. Stir well, using a wooden spoon to scrape up any spices sticking to the bottom of the pot. Add 360 ml / 1½ cups of water, stir well, and reduce the heat to low. Cook for an hour, until the beef is tender. Whenever the water level decreases, add another 120 ml / ½ cup. (It seems like my great-grandmother used to say to add a teacup's worth. But a teacup's worth is a bit like all other measurements from grandmothers—a pinch, or a handful—which are very subjective. Teacups range from small porcelain teacups to large teacups. Nevertheless, add water and stir to make sure that nothing sticks to the bottom.)

After 45 to 60 minutes, a bit of sauce should form at the bottom of the pot. If not, add another 120 ml / ½ cup water and bring it to a boil while stirring to end up with a thick sauce and the delicious Rosto Mariam.

PURSLANE DIP

100 g / 2 cups purslane
2 tablespoons extra-virgin
    olive oil
2 spring onions (scallions),
    finely chopped
¼ teaspoon salt
20 g / ½ cup mint leaves
Bread, preferably kmaj or
    flatbread, to serve

SERVES 2 TO 4

Purslane, with its rounded, thick leaves, is available in late spring and summer in Palestine. It's a popular find on dining tables. It is the original component of fattoush salad—a bread salad—which traditionally didn't include lettuce, but would be made with purslane.

I discovered this combination a while back, and I have been enjoying it ever since. Purslane has a delicate earthy taste and, when it is in season, I always add it to as many salads and combinations as I can.

Pull the purslane leaves off the stems and discard the stems.

In a frying pan over medium heat, heat 1 tablespoon of the olive oil. Add the purslane and sauté for 3 to 4 minutes, until tender.

Mix the purslane and the spring onions in a bowl and add the salt. Refrigerate for 1 hour.

To serve, transfer the purslane mixture to a plate. Tear the mint leaves by hand and add to the middle of the plate. Drizzle the remaining 1 tablespoon of olive oil on top. Serve with bread for dipping.

YAKHNI
BAMIA

Olive oil
2 onions, 1 finely chopped,
    1 diced
Salt
500 g / 18 ounces lamb
    shoulder, cut into
    medium-size cubes
½ teaspoon black pepper
4 ripe tomatoes, diced
2 bay leaves
1 cinnamon stick
4 cardamom pods
400 g / 14 ounces
    tomato sauce
240 ml / 1 cup water plus
    warm water as needed
10 garlic cloves, 6 crushed,
    4 left whole
2 bunches of coriander
    (fresh cilantro), finely
    chopped
800 g / 1¾ pounds okra,
    the smallest size, either
    fresh or frozen and
    thawed, trimmed
½ teaspoon ground cumin
½ lemon
Hot cooked rice, to serve

SERVES 6

Bamia, or okra, is one of my favorite vegetables, and I think it is very underrated. We have a preconception that people either hate or love bamia, because of its particular texture. When cooked, okra can be a bit gooey, to a point where it's often not served to foreign guests, the advice might be to not cook bamia for them. Instead, I make it my intention to try to convince as many people as possible of its wonderful texture and taste.

Different sizes and types of okra are already enjoyed in large parts of the world, particularly in African and Asian communities. In Palestine, about mid-May to the beginning of June when the weather is warm, bamia pops up in the market. I wait for this time because I love to play with bamia recipes.

I sometimes deep fry it like chips with a little spice; other times I make it the traditional way. Years ago, I had the fun experience of cooking bamia with Mohamad Hadid, a Palestinian-American originally from Nazareth and Safad. His mother's recipe is quite close to my family's, which I offer here, despite her being from the north of the country and having lived in exile since 1948.

Heat 2 tablespoons olive oil in a large pot over medium heat. Add the finely chopped onion and ¼ teaspoon salt. Cook and stir until the onion is soft, 3 to 5 minutes. Add the lamb and the pepper, and brown the cubes, turning and stirring, for 5 to 6 minutes. Add the tomatoes and stir well for 2 minutes. Add the bay leaves, cinnamon stick, cardamom, and 200 g / 7 ounces of the tomato sauce. Add the water and leave to cook for 40 minutes over medium heat.

Meanwhile, in a deep pan, heat another 2 tablespoons olive oil over medium heat. Add the diced onion, crushed garlic cloves, and half the coriander. Sauté until the onion is translucent, about 5 minutes.

Add the okra, cumin, and ¼ teaspoon salt. Sauté, stirring for about 10 minutes, until the okra is cooked through and golden. Add the remaining 200 g / 7 ounces tomato sauce and cook for 5 to 7 minutes, until the okra is tender but not mushy. If required to prevent sticking, add up to 120 ml / ½ cup of warm water.

With a slotted spoon, transfer the lamb into the pot with the okra. Pour the liquid from the pot with the meat through a sieve and over the meat until the liquid in the pot has the consistency of a stew. Decrease the heat and continue to cook for 10 to 12 minutes, until the lamb and okra are soft.

Meanwhile, in a small pan, heat 1 tablespoon olive oil over medium heat. Add the remaining coriander and whole garlic cloves and fry until the garlic is coloured, about 3 minutes. This is called the *tasha.* Add it to the stew. Add a squeeze of the lemon and serve with a side of rice.

ROASTED GREEN CHICKPEAS

Juice of 1 lemon
1½ teaspoons salt
¼ teaspoon dried red
pepper flakes
¼ teaspoon hot paprika
400 g / 3 cups fresh green
chickpeas in the pod

SERVES 4

As soon as green chickpeas appear in Palestinian markets, there is a frenzy of shoppers. Like a lot of other products, they have a short season. In carts across the city, they are also sold grilled. My uncle Abdallah and his wife, May, always make sure to take advantage of the availability of the chickpeas and roast them at home as often as they can. As a kid, I would sometimes go to study at their house and my uncle would help me with chemistry, his specialty. I knew that when the chickpeas were in season, that would be the best time to visit them.

I've added my own twist to this recipe. However, it has the same smell and taste that you would find in any Palestinian home. This is a simple snack that everybody enjoys in Palestine.

Preheat the grill (broiler).

In a bowl, mix together the lemon juice, salt, red pepper flakes, and paprika. Add the chickpeas and mix well. Evenly spread out the chickpeas on a baking sheet, making sure they are in a single layer, to evenly roast.

Broil until they are roasted and crispy, giving them a stir when the top starts colouring, 5 to 7 minutes total. Enjoy them hot or cooled. I prefer them to be slightly cooled, with the beans still warm.

DIBS AND TAHINIA SHORT-BREAD

This is a distinctive biscuit with a nutty, slightly fruity taste that is reminiscent of childhood for Palestinians raised with dibs o tahinia (see page 14). Traditionally, dibs (grape molasses) is mixed with tahinia in equal parts to make the creamy sweet dip for bread, usually for breakfast. This was a favourite of Baba Fuad, always on his breakfast table.

The dough here is a crumbly one, so be sure to use it chilled. This recipe makes about 30 biscuits, which will last for several days, but I promise they will quickly disappear.

150 g / 9 tablespoons salted butter, at room temperature, chopped
100 g / ½ cup demerara sugar (or substitute another raw sugar)
100 g / ⅓ cup dibs
175 g / ½ cup plus 1½ teaspoons tahinia
300 g / 2½ cups all-purpose flour, plus more for the work surface
½ teaspoon baking powder

MAKES 30 BISCUITS (COOKIES)

In a mixing bowl, combine the butter, sugar, dibs, and tahinia. Mix with a handheld beater for 5 minutes, until smooth.

In a separate bowl, whisk together the flour and baking powder.

With the beater on low speed, add the flour mixture gradually into the tahinia mixture until smooth.

Turn the dough out onto a floured surface and knead for 5 minutes, until smooth. Divide the dough into two portions, place each in a bowl, cover with plastic wrap, and chill in refrigerator for 1 to 2 hours.

Preheat the oven to 180°C / 350°F. Line two baking sheets with parchment paper.

Working with one portion of dough at a time, roll out the dough on a floured surface until it is ½ to 1 cm / ¼ to ⅜ inch thick. Use a cookie cutter to cut out biscuits, and place them on the prepared sheet, leaving about 2½ cm / 1 inch between the biscuits. Repeat with the second portion of dough.

Bake, one sheet at a time, for 12 to 15 minutes, until the biscuits are golden brown and firm to the touch. Allow to cool on the sheets. Store in an airtight container for 4 to 5 days.

BARBECUED WHOLE CHICKEN

The sight of mouthwatering charcoal-grilled barbecued chicken is common in Palestine. On sunny days, every household begins barbecuing whole chickens marinated in beautiful local flavors. At the same time, in every town, there is at least one restaurant renowned for its barbecued chicken. In Bethlehem, it is Qabar restaurant in Beit Jala. It was established in 1974 and is still one of the most popular places. I grew up going there to pick up some chicken to bring home to enjoy with bread and a simple salad.

80 ml / ⅓ cup extra-virgin olive oil, plus more as needed
60 ml / ¼ cup fresh lemon juice
6 garlic cloves, crushed
1 teaspoon salt
1 tablespoon ground sumac
1 teaspoon dried red pepper flakes
½ teaspoon ground cumin
¼ teaspoon ground cinnamon
¼ teaspoon ground allspice
Peel of 1 white or black loumi (dried lime), grated with a Microplane
1 whole chicken, about 1½ kg / 3⅓ pounds, spatchcocked

TO FINISH
3 garlic cloves, crushed
1 green chilli, sliced
2 tablespoons olive oil
Juice of 1 lemon
1 teaspoon ground sumac

SERVES 4

In a large nonreactive bowl, mix together the olive oil, lemon juice, garlic, salt, sumac, red pepper flakes, cumin, cinnamon, allspice, and grated loumi. Add the chicken and rub the mix all over it. If you don't plan to barbecue immediately, cover the bowl and refrigerate overnight.

To barbecue on a charcoal or gas grill, prepare the grill with a hot zone and a cooler zone. Place the chicken, skin side up, on the cooler side, with the legs facing the hotter side. Cover the grill and cook until the chicken is mostly done, 40 to 45 minutes. Carefully flip the chicken and place it on the hotter side of the grill, skin side down, to crisp the skin and finish cooking the chicken, another 10 to 15 minutes. It should take 50 to 60 minutes total.

To cook in the oven, preheat the oven to 220°C / 425°F. Preheat a skillet over medium-high heat on the stove.

Put the chicken in the skillet, skin side up. Sear for about 4 minutes, then flip the chicken over. Sear on the second side for about 4 minutes. Continue flipping the chicken until you have charred the skin.

Transfer the chicken to a baking sheet, skin side up, add a drizzle of olive oil, and roast for another 25 to 30 minutes, to fully cook through.

Remove from the heat of the grill or oven and let rest for 10 minutes.

Meanwhile, in a bowl, mix together the garlic, chilli, olive oil, lemon juice, and sumac. Drizzle over the chicken, cut into pieces, and serve.

MOUHALABIEH

Mouhalabieh, or milk pudding, is a creamy, fragrant dessert that transports you with each mouthful to Palestine. The light taste of mastic is ideal for joining the flavours from across the Palestinian terroir.

Served chilled, with dates studded with cloves from Gaza, ripe fruit from Bethlehem, or a few candied oranges from Jaffa, mouhalabieh is an ideal dessert for all seasons.

750 ml / 3⅛ cups whole milk (or substitute almond milk)
120 g / 1 cup sugar
1 teaspoon ground mastic
80 g / ½ cup cornstarch
Finely chopped pistachios, to garnish

SERVES 6 TO 8

Heat about two-thirds of the milk with the sugar and mastic in a pot over medium heat. Meanwhile, whisk the cornstarch and the remaining milk in a bowl until smooth. Slowly add the cornstarch mixture to the pot, stirring continuously with a wooden spoon and making sure the milk doesn't stick to the bottom.

Once the pudding thickens, remove it from the heat, stir well, and pour into glass serving bowls. Let cool at room temperature for 1 hour. Chill in the refrigerator for a minimum of 2 hours.

Garnish with the pistachios and serve.

ORANGES AND ROSES WITH TETA EMILY

I never had a chance to meet my paternal grandmother, Emily, but traces of her adventures, interests, and passions always surrounded me and have made their way into my kitchen.

I grew up visiting the historic stone house where I now live, to see my grandfather, Nakhleh. This was once Emily's home, too, and even though she passed away in 1967, a full decade before I was born, her memory has never faded. Sido Nakhleh loved to tell tales of their lives together, and my maternal grandmother, Julia, who happened to be Emily's sister, was another well of stories. There are faded images of Emily which have always tantalised me. Photographs offer glimpses of her living in Kobe, Japan, early on in her married life, until World War II forced my grandparents to leave in 1943. There are photos of Emily in Bombay, where my father was born. However, the ones that most affect me show Emily in Palestine. I treasure pictures of her in our sizeable orange groves in Jaffa, which were lost in the Nakba (catastrophe) of 1948.

In one photograph Emily is smiling widely while touching her wide-brimmed hat as the Palestinian sun beats down. In another, she sits with her siblings by a pool surrounded by lush trees, enjoying her oranges, just months before the land was lost overnight.

The relationship with the land is built into the memory of its people. Jaffa oranges, most notably the Shamouti variety, famous for their vivid colour and sweetness, are part of our rich history and heritage. The oranges were internationally exported and were for decades a source of great pride and wealth. Each family that was involved in the successful trade has its own story, but little of ours has been passed onto my generation. It always felt like speaking about this loss was too painful. I still have the land ownership documents which Sido Nakhleh carefully filed in the family archive, and I wonder how he and Teta Emily dealt with the nostalgia and whether they expected to ever return to their stolen groves.

Like so many Palestinians, I always feel a deep sense of longing and hope for justice. While as Bethlehemites, my family was not forcibly displaced from our hometown, plunged into the uncertain fate of refugees, we still had our losses. In a sense these losses are common to all Palestinian families—with their various memories of oranges, olive trees, prickly pears, and fishermen's boats. The planning archives of pre-1948 Jaffa are not publicly accessible, so I have never been able to link our deeds to an exact location there. This leaves me staring uselessly at photographs for clues. My grandmother's oranges have taken on a mythical status for me. I wish I knew if the groves still exist, if there is someone picking the juicy fruits this season or sinking their teeth into one right now.

For me, the tangy flavour of Jaffa oranges will always be associated with Emily's carefree smile. Memories of both work their way in when I am preparing one of my Teta Julia's signature recipes. Her Clementine Givree—a staple of New Year's Eve dinner menus—is the dessert that I most enjoy making, especially for big occasions and family get-togethers.

The magically uplifting fragrance of roses is also inextricably linked to Teta Emily. After all, I spent years as a child running around on land which she had planted with rosebushes long before I was born. I was always told that she loved these brightly coloured flowers, and I have continued to tend them and plant new ones for her in the garden by the house over the years. After opening my restaurant Fawda in Bethlehem, I became obsessed with trying out rose varieties that I could grow organically and sustainably. I loved to create desserts that used fresh edible petals and would secretly smile as I did so, thinking of each of these dishes from Bethlehem as an homage to my Teta Emily.

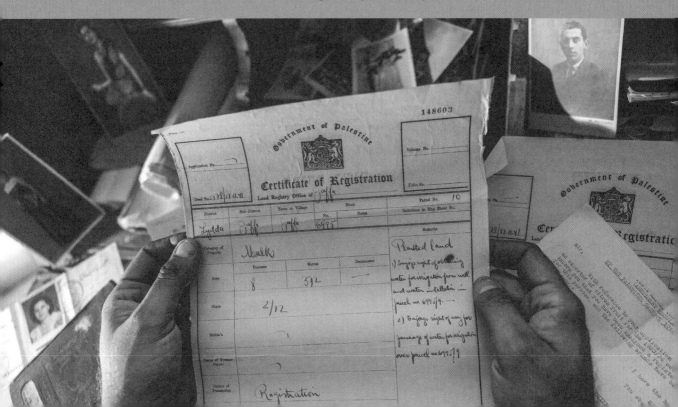

STUFFED COURGETTE FLOWERS

In summer, when the small green courgettes (zucchini) are in season and they arrive at the markets ready for *mahshi* (to be cored and stuffed), they often have their sunny yellow blossoms still attached to them, but we do not use these much in Palestine. Years ago, at Fawda, when I used to buy courgettes, I would be like a kid in a candy shop with all those beautiful courgette flowers available, and I would stuff them with baladi cheese (a fresh local cheese of cow, sheep, and goat milk) and deep-fry them. They would be a perfect accompaniment for a drink or as an amuse-bouche.

1 egg
125 g / 1 cup all-purpose
    flour
1 tablespoon extra-virgin
    olive oil
1 tablespoon milk
8 courgette flowers
    (zucchini blossoms)
130 g / 4½ ounces baladi
    or Nabulsi cheese
    (soaked and drained
    to remove some
    salt), or substitute
    another brined cheese,
    crumbled
1 tablespoon chopped
    fresh flat-leaf parsley
    leaves
1 teaspoon nigella seeds
400 ml / 1⅔ cups
    vegetable oil or
    sunflower oil

To make the batter, in a large bowl, whisk the egg. While continuing to whisk, add the flour, olive oil, and the milk. Leave to rest for an hour at room temperature.

Open the courgette flowers carefully and remove the pistils.

In a small bowl, combine the cheese, parsley, and nigella and mix well. Stuff the flowers with this mixture and pinch the tips of the flowers closed to keep the stuffing in.

In a medium-size frying pan, heat the vegetable oil over high heat. Once the oil is hot, after 2 to 3 minutes, decrease the heat to medium.

Working in batches, dip the stuffed courgette flowers in the batter, then carefully slip them into the hot oil; don't crowd the pan. Fry until golden on each side, about 2 minutes. Remove from the oil and place them on paper towels to drain. Serve immediately.

SERVES 8

AUBERGINE SALAD WITH TAHINIA

Aubergines (eggplant) are an essential part of the Palestinian diet, especially celebrated in such places such as Battir, a village to the west of Bethlehem. It is known far and wide for having the best aubergines, and its name is synonymous with a long, thin purple variety. The different-size aubergines are used differently in Palestinian cuisine. Small aubergines are pickled and stuffed with crunchy walnuts, garlic, and carrots to make makdous. The medium-size ones are stuffed with rice and meat, while the large size is used for makloubeh (see page 179), baba ghanoush, or salads. I am obsessed with sumac and its distinctive taste. So, this recipe balances the sweetness of the aubergines, the intensity of the tahinia, and the tanginess of the sumac.

3 tablespoons extra-virgin olive oil
2 large aubergines, cut into 1 cm / ⅜-inch cubes
1 onion, thinly sliced
4 garlic cloves
½ teaspoon salt
3 tablespoons tahinia
Juice of 2 lemons
1½ teaspoons ground sumac
Up to 120 ml / ½ cup water
20 g / ¾ ounce laban jameed (salted and dried yoghurt) (or substitute a cheese of your liking, despite laban jameed not being a cheese)
A few mint leaves

SERVES 4 TO 6

In a large skillet over high heat, warm 2 tablespoons of the olive oil. Add the aubergines and onion and sauté. Decrease the heat once the eggplants are golden and cook until the aubergines are soft all the way through.

To make the sauce, crush the garlic with the salt. Transfer to a bowl and whisk in the tahinia. Whisk in the lemon juice. Mix in the sumac. Dilute the mixture with water until the sauce is liquid enough to coat the aubergines.

In a mixing bowl, toss the cooked aubergines and onions with the sauce, coating them well.

Sprinkle the laban jameed over the top. Rub the mint leaves between your hands to release their flavour, then sprinkle on top. Drizzle the remaining 1 tablespoon of olive oil on top. Serve at once or store in the fridge and serve later.

FIG JAM

1 kg / 2¼ pounds figs,
   halved and stemmed
400 g / 2 cups sugar
25 g / 2 tablespoons
   ground sumac
Juice of 1 lemon
100 g / 1 cup whole peeled
   pistachios

**MAKES THREE
250 ML / 1 CUP JARS**

From a simple basket of fresh figs, to roasted figs, to a slice of fig in a labaneh (strained and seasoned yoghurt) sandwich, figs are a game changer.

The season of figs brings on all those sublime juicy green, black, and purple figs—the best being the ones you pick from the tree yourself and bite into. Those delicious flavours of fig bring colour and sunshine to my table all summer long.

A few years ago, I was experimenting with a fig jam and some sumac, when my cousin Jumana and I decided to start a small collaboration for her brand in Jordan, Kama. As you can imagine, this jam recipe was the first to end up in the range of jams we produced.

In a bowl, mix together the figs and sugar, gently coating the figs. Add the sumac and mix well, but gently, so as not to crush the fruit. Leave to macerate at cool room temperature for 1 to 2 hours, until the fruit releases some juices. Transfer to a heavy pot.

Over high heat, bring the fig mixture to a boil, stirring continuously. Boil for 5 minutes, making sure the sugar and fig juices don't scorch on the bottom. Decrease the heat, add the lemon juice, and cook for 30 minutes. The fruit will cook down to almost a jam consistency, but some of the fruit will remain whole. Continue cooking until the jam reaches a temperature of 105°C / 220°F on an instant-read thermometer. Add the pistachios and remove from the heat.

Transfer the hot jam to sterilized jars, cover, and let cool to room temperature.

Store the jam in the refrigerator.

SHAWARMA

Shawarma is another iconic Palestinian street food. Drive along any Palestinian main street, and you will see the skewers slowly rotating in shops and shawarma vendors slicing away. But you can also make a fantastic sandwich at home with meat, spices, and simple toppings. Just anticipating it will make your mouth water. Below I provide two ways to cook the meat: on the stove or in the oven.

MEAT AND MARINADE
1 kg / 2½ pounds bavette steak
6 garlic cloves, crushed
1 teaspoon salt
1 teaspoon ground allspice
½ teaspoon ground cinnamon
½ teaspoon ground cardamom
½ teaspoon ground cumin
½ teaspoon ground mastic
¼ teaspoon ground chilli powder
¼ teaspoon ground nutmeg
¼ teaspoon ground ginger
120 ml / ½ cup fresh lemon juice
60 ml / ¼ cup white wine vinegar
60 ml / ¼ cup extra-virgin olive oil
Vegetable oil

TAHINIA SAUCE
120 ml / ½ cup fresh lemon juice
2 garlic cloves
2 teaspoons tahinia
½ teaspoon salt
120 ml / ½ cup water

TO SERVE
8 half pitas, shrak, or flatbreads
Green Shatta (page 76)
Pickled cucumber slices
Onion slices

SERVES 8

To prepare the meat, cut the steak into thin strips about 8 to 10 cm / 3 to 4 inches long and a bit thicker than a julienne cut.

To make the marinade, in a large bowl, mix together the garlic, salt, allspice, cinnamon, cardamom, cumin, mastic, chilli powder, nutmeg, and ginger. Stir in the lemon juice, vinegar, and olive oil. Add the meat and mix so all the pieces are well coated. Cover and marinate in the fridge overnight.

The next day, take the meat out of the fridge and allow it to sit at room temperature for at least a half hour.

To cook the beef on the stovetop, heat a large frying pan over medium-high heat with a dash of vegetable oil. Drain the meat and reserve the marinade. Lay a single layer of beef strips in the pan and cook until browned on both sides, 8 to 10 minutes. Just before you remove the beef from the pan, add a spoonful of the reserved marinade and stir well so the meat gets coated with the juices. Repeat with the remaining meat until it is all cooked.

To cook the meat in the oven, preheat the oven to 150°C / 300°F. Line a roasting pan or baking sheet with parchment paper. Lay the meat strips in the pan and spoon a bit of the marinade over the top. Cover the pan and bake for about 1¾ hours. Uncover the pan, increase the oven temperature to 200°C / 400°F, and cook for another 15 minutes, so the meat gets a bit crisp.

While the meat is cooking, prepare the tahinia sauce. In a blender, combine the lemon juice, garlic, tahinia, and salt and process until blended. With the blender running, slowly add the water. It should make a creamy sauce.

To assemble the shawarmas, take a pita and spread a bit of the tahinia sauce on it. Add the meat, the shatta for a spicy kick, and a few slices of pickled cucumber and onion. Repeat as needed to use all the ingredients. *Sahtain!*

WATERMELON SALAD

Summer in Palestine without watermelon and Nabulsi cheese doesn't count as summer.

Watermelon became highly symbolic in Palestinian modern culture when, after the occupation of the West Bank, East Jerusalem, and Gaza in 1967, Israel made it illegal to carry the Palestinian flag. In the early 1980s, Palestinian artist Sliman Mansour circumvented this ban by painting the watermelon, its colours being the same as those of the flag.

As soon as the first watermelons arrive at the market, everybody starts queuing up to buy them, along with Nabulsi cheese, for the ideal evening snack on the hot nights of Bethlehem. In Palestine, it is known that the best watermelons come from Jenin. I think a watermelon salad can go perfectly well for breakfast, lunch, or dinner. When temperatures rise above 30°C / 86°F, it is always a welcome, refreshing dish.

150 g / 5¼ ounces Nabulsi cheese (or substitute another brined cheese)
2½ tablespoons extra-virgin olive oil
2 tablespoons almonds
2 tablespoons fresh lemon juice
2 tablespoons fresh mint leaves
2 tablespoons fresh flat-leaf parsley leaves
½ red or green chilli, sliced into rings
600 g / 1⅓ pounds diced watermelon
180 g / 6¼ ounces tomatoes, halved and cut into slivers
120 g / 4¼ ounces cucumber, cut into batons
90 g / 3¼ ounces pitted cured black olives

SERVES 4 TO 6

Remove the Nabulsi cheese from its brine, if it has been stored in it. Place it in a bowl with water to cover and change the water a couple of times to reduce the saltiness of the cheese. Drain well. Dice the cheese, aiming for the same size as the watermelon cubes or a bit smaller.

In a small pan, heat 1½ teaspoons of the olive oil over medium heat. Add the almonds and toast until golden, 3 minutes. Set aside.

Prepare the dressing by mixing together the remaining 2 tablespoons olive oil, the lemon juice, and a little bit of the mint and parsley leaves.

In a bowl, combine the cheese, chilli, watermelon, tomatoes, cucumbers, and olives. Add the dressing and toss gently.

To serve, transfer the salad to a serving bowl. Sprinkle the remaining mint and parsley and the toasted almonds on top. The salad can be made in advance and refrigerated to allow the flavors to mix. However, it's better if it's made on the spot.

BRAISED SILEK WITH TAHINIA

Silek (chard) can be sautéed in olive oil with garlic, cooked with meat, or used in place of grape leaves. In Gaza, it is often combined with sumac, red tahinia, and lamb meat to make sumaqqiyeh. This is my take on that dish, with a vegetarian approach. Though ground from the same sesame seeds as its paler cousins, red tahinia is made from sesame seeds that are slow-roasted in giant ovens and stirred often. This yields its signature reddish tint.

20 g / ½ cup dried sumac
   berries
2 tablespoons extra-virgin
   olive oil
1 onion, finely chopped
3 garlic cloves, crushed
2 teaspoons salt
3 bunches silek (chard),
   stalks and leaves
   separated and chopped
4 tablespoons fresh lemon
   juice
1 tablespoon dill seeds
1 green chilli, chopped
   finely
1 teaspoon coriander seeds
3 tablespoons tahinia

**CARAMELISED
ONION GARNISH**
2 tablespoons olive oil
1 onion, finely chopped

SERVES 4 TO 6

Cover the sumac berries with water in a small saucepan and bring to a boil over medium-high heat. Set aside for 30 minutes, then pass through a fine sieve, keeping the liquid and discarding the solids.

In a large pot over medium heat, warm the olive oil. Add the onion and two-thirds of the garlic, the salt, and the silek stalks, stir, and cook for about 8 minutes, until softened. Add the silek leaves, 2 tablespoons of the lemon juice, 1½ teaspoons of the dill seeds, the green chilli, coriander seeds, and sumac-infused water. Cover and braise for 10 to 12 minutes, until tender.

Remove the silek leaves from the cooking water. Pass the cooking water through a fine-mesh sieve into a bowl and dispose of any solids.

To make the sauce, mix the tahinia, remaining lemon juice, garlic, and 1½ teaspoons dill seeds. Slowly add the red-tinted cooking water to the tahinia sauce to thin the sauce to a pouring consistency.

To make the caramelised onion garnish, in a small pan over medium heat, combine the olive oil and onion. Sauté for 15 to 20 minutes to caramelise.

To serve, place the braised silek in a bowl, drizzle the tahinia sauce on top, and garnish with caramelised onions. Enjoy!

AUTUMN

MISTAKA BRIOCHE

I grew up with stories of my late grandmother, Emily, whom I never got to meet, baking a fragrant mastic brioche with bright red–coloured eggs baked in the middle as an Easter treat for my father and his siblings when they were young in Bethlehem. I remember enjoying such brioches sent to us by family friends from Jerusalem. The smell and taste are so evocative. I started making the mastic brioche without the egg, all year round. My favorite way to enjoy this bread is with a bit of butter and quince jam.

2½ teaspoons dry baker's yeast
80 g / 6½ tablespoons sugar
200 ml / ¾ cup plus 2 tablespoons lukewarm milk
500 g / 4 cups plus 3 tablespoons all-purpose flour, plus more for the work surface
2 eggs
1 tablespoon orange blossom water
½ teaspoon salt
½ teaspoon ground mastic
100 g / ½ cup unsalted butter, at room temperature, cut into small cubes

EGG WASH
1 egg yolk
1 tablespoon milk

MAKES 1 LOAF

In a small bowl, mix together the yeast, 40 g / 3 tablespoons of the sugar, and 50 ml / 3½ tablespoons of the milk. Set aside until it foams, about 10 minutes.

In the bowl of a stand mixer fitted with a dough hook, combine the flour, the remaining sugar, and the remaining milk. Mix at low speed until the ingredients are combined. Add the eggs, orange blossom water, salt, and mastic. Continue to mix at low speed for 8 minutes. Increase the speed and beat for another 5 minutes. Add the butter and beat for another 8 minutes.

Scoop out pieces of dough with your hand and form into rounded shapes. Set aside on a lightly floured work surface. Cover and leave to rise for 1 hour.

Grease a 23 cm / 9-inch round cake pan. Press the rounded pieces gently to remove the gas that has formed. Put the dough pieces in the pan, cover, and let rise for 45 to 60 minutes, until doubled in size.

Preheat the oven to 180°C / 350°F.

To make the egg wash, mix the egg yolk and milk until well blended. Brush over the dough without pressing on the tops.

Bake for 20 to 25 minutes, until the top of the brioche is brown. Lightly cover with aluminum foil or parchment paper and continue to bake for 20 to 25 minutes, until the brioche sounds hollow when tapped and reads 90°C / 190°F in the centre with an instant-read thermometer.

Transfer the brioche from the cake pan to a rack and leave to cool before digging in.

LAHMET HATOUM

In my great-grandmother's generation, all the cooks in the family had their own twists on lamb and beef stews. This lamb stew is a recipe made by one of the cousins, Hatoum, and widely adopted in the family. It has a very particular zing that's added at the end of the cooking, which makes it a bit unusual and yet very much loved.

The home of that cousin is on the same street as my great-grandparents' house in the Old City of Bethlehem. The street is adjacent to the souk and the butcher's market is next door, so you can imagine how fresh the meat they were using was. They would literally cross the street to pick up their lamb.

1 tablespoon plus
1 teaspoon samneh (ghee)
1 kg / 2¼ pounds boneless lamb, cut into cubes
9 garlic cloves
1 teaspoon allspice
¼ teaspoon ground cinnamon
¼ teaspoon ground coriander
¼ teaspoon ground cumin
¼ teaspoon ground cardamom
¼ teaspoon ground nutmeg
¼ teaspoon ground cloves
Salt and ground black pepper
Water
1 hot green chilli
Juice of 2 lemons

In a large pot, melt 1 tablespoon of the samneh over medium-high heat. Add the lamb cubes and sear on all sides for about 10 minutes, until well-browned.

Crush 4 of the garlic cloves and add to the lamb along with the allspice, cinnamon, coriander, cumin, cardamom, nutmeg, and cloves. Season with salt and pepper and stir for 2 to 3 minutes, until the meat is well coated.

Add water to cover the lamb and bring to a boil. Then decrease the heat to simmer. Taste the broth and add more salt and pepper, if needed.

Cover the pot and leave it to cook for about 45 minutes, until the lamb is tender and cooked through and the juices of the broth have reduced to practically a sauce.

Meanwhile, in a mortar, crush the remaining 5 cloves of garlic with the chilli and mix in the lemon juice. Melt the remaining 1 teaspoon of samneh and mix it in. Pour over the meat and the sauce while they are still simmering, stir, and simmer for 4 to 5 minutes longer. Then it is ready to be served!

SERVES 4 TO 6

PALESTINIAN PICKLED OLIVES

Pickled olives are a staple on every Palestinian table for breakfast, lunch, and dinner. They go into sandwiches and salads, but for me, olives are best served alone with some hot fresh bread—a mouthful of pure delight to savour. A lot of Palestinians have olive trees in front of their houses or in their own family grove. Some villages survive mainly on their production of olive oil and pickled olives. And each of those locations prides itself on having the best olive oil and olives. As soon as we Palestinians have a bit of land, the first thing we do is plant an olive tree. I was fortunate enough to plant a few trees years ago and today enjoy making pickled olives from them every season. The exact recipe for pickling changes from one family to another, but the results are more or less the same.

1 kg / 2¼ pounds fresh green olives (make sure the olives haven't been dented while being picked)
500 g / 3½ cups coarse salt, plus 1½ tablespoons for each 240 ml / 1 cup of water in the brine
500 g / 1⅛ pounds lemons
3 to 4 green chillies
Olive oil
Fresh or brined grape leaves

MAKES TWO 500 G / 1 PINT JARS

Wash and dry the olives. Traditionally the olives are crushed with a mortar, but you can score them with a knife on both sides. Cover the olives with water and set aside for 3 days, changing the water daily.

After 3 days, drain off the water. Coat the olives with the salt. Set aside for 2 days, draining off any excess water during this time.

On the fifth day, slice the lemons and chillies into wheels. Place in a bowl and mix together. Drain the olives and mix with the lemons and chillies.

Fill sterilized jars with olives, lemon slices and chilli slices. To make the brine, for each jar, combine 240 ml / 1 cup water with 1½ tablespoons salt. Fill up the jars with brine. Add a tablespoon of olive oil to each jar. Place a few grape leaves on top to seal the jars.

Close the jars and store them in a dark, dry area for a month. They will last up to a year unopened.

SPICES WITH TAWFIK LAMA

On Bethlehem's historic Star Street, a short walk from Manger Square—both part of a UNESCO World Heritage Site—there is a tiny shop that celebrates our rich culinary inheritance. I just open the door of Orient Mills, a store founded by the Lama family way back in 1936, and I am transported back in time by the intoxicating medley of scents: freshly roasted coffee, zaatar, sumac, pepper, and incense. My grandmother Julia was a regular customer. After she set up a museum nearby with a group of Bethlehemite women in the 1970s (see page 186), she would go there most afternoons and would often pass by Orient Mills, too. When I was small, I would accompany her and absorb all the delicious smells of those spices.

Years later, I set up Fawda, my restaurant in Bethlehem, just off the same street, within easy reach of Orient Mills. It is a chef's dream to have a spice master close by at all times, and it has meant that I keep only minimal stocks of spices. I have the delight of being able to buy what I need freshly ground, from day to day. Tawfik Lama and I even have our own rituals. Whenever I walk into his shop and find him busily serving customers, I head behind the counter to the back of the store where I sit on the wooden steps that lead to his storage area and wait my turn. Tawfik will hand me a cup of coffee to enjoy with a cigarette while I watch him and his assistant, Mohammad, at work. It always impresses me that they have memorised how their regulars like their Arabic coffee—the exact ratio of dark- and light-roasted beans with cardamom added to taste. The little store has three noisy coffee grinders constantly whirring away.

In the neatly arranged glass jars, you will find all the classic Palestinian spices. There is the familiar ground sumac found in every local kitchen. It has a sour, tangy taste. You'll also find whole dried red sumac berries. In Palestine, the best come from Hebron. I often soak these and use their juice in a reduction to finish dishes or create sumaqqiyeh. You will also find zaatar mix, another very popular and common staple of every Palestinian breakfast table. It is delicious eaten with bread that has first been dipped in olive oil. Like the coffee, the zaatar mix is a matter of personal preference. It consists of the dried green leaves of the zaatar plant that grows wild around Bethlehem which I used to pick with my grandmother—plus sumac with a hint of salt. These are ground together with toasted sesame seeds added on top. Another common purchase is the aromatic blend simply referred to as seven spice, which is familiar to every Palestinian cook. This consists of ground allspice, black pepper, coriander, cumin, cloves, and nutmeg, with cinnamon or cardamom. Tawfik grinds all of these every few days so that customers can make their own mix rich in flavour.

My favourite shelf in the shop bears the ingredients that were historically used in Palestinian cuisine but are now far less popular. I love the little black pine seeds that awaken more childhood memories. I used to search under the pine trees for the cones that they came from, so that I could crack them open and remove their tiny treasures. Incense sticks, including frankincense, are also found here. These are still used by Bethlehemites to take to church as an offering or to burn in their homes, but I sometimes use them in my cooking. I have developed a crème anglaise that is infused with this scent.

Tawfik is a kind man who will sometimes accompany me in my crazy creative pursuits. When I first insisted on trying to figure out how to use the woody, sweet, and citrusy aroma of frankincense in a dish, we decided to use the hinge of his outside metal door to burn the incense with coal under it, so that

we were not overcome by the smell in the store. Over the course of a few hours, a section of Star Street was full of the scent, and we were drawing the amused attention of other shopkeepers. Some still like to remind us of this strange behaviour today.

Tawfik also sells my favourite grain, freekeh, a green durum wheat that is charred with the burnt outer husk rubbed off. It can be cooked like rice but has a distinctive smoky flavour and a delicious al dente texture. For me, the best freekeh comes from the northern West Bank. Tawfik sources his from around Jenin.

Like other Bethlehemites, I might drop into the store for falafel spices or samneh (ghee) when my homemade stocks run out. There are also wonderful ingredients that you will struggle to find elsewhere, such as loumi—dried black limes packed with intense flavour—and dried lemons.

At festive times, the shop starts selling mahlab, the ground and dried pits of sour cherry, and mistaka (mastic). That is how I register that we are getting close to Easter, Christmas, Ramadan, Eid al-Adha, or Eid al-Fitr. Palestinians celebrate all of these with ka'ek (sesame bread) and ma'amoul, a mouthwatering butter pastry made with semolina flour and stuffed with date paste or walnuts. A specific feast which I especially enjoy celebrating is that of Saint Barbara on December 4 and 17, observed by all the Christian denominations. This is when we make a toothsome, porridge-like warm dessert called burbara (page 205). While making his preparations, Tawfik gives over a corner of his store to the ingredients: the wheat berries, spices, sheets of dried apricot paste called kamardin, dried fruits, nuts, and candied anise and fennel. This has been the routine since the shop opened in 1936, and I find that continuity deeply reassuring.

Needless to say, when I started giving Palestinian cuisine tours in Bethlehem, Tawfik's shop was always on the map. He offered coffee to our guests and talked passionately about his spices. Nobody ever goes home without some zaatar, sumac, freekeh, and mahlab. Some they might buy, but Tawfik can never resist packaging up extra gifts, too. For me, he represents the essence of Bethlehem's hospitality. Tawfik is rightly proud of his craft and enjoys sharing the knowledge that has been passed down through generations of his family. In the face of challenges from all of our social changes, he continues to sell first-rate products.

LOUKMET SHISH BARAK

Shish barak are little Palestinian dumplings filled with lamb and boiled, then cooked in sauces made with laban jameed (salted and dried yoghurt). I've played around with recipes for shish barak, with different flavors and accompaniments, in both of my restaurants, Fawda and Akub. *Loukmeh* means "mouthful" in Arabic, so here I recommend a serving of three little dumplings—three little bites per person, more or less—depending on where it is placed in a meal.

DOUGH
70 g / ½ cup all-purpose flour, plus more for the work surface and baking sheet
Salt
1½ teaspoons extra-virgin olive oil, plus more for the baking sheet
120 ml / ½ cup water

FILLING
1 tablespoon extra-virgin olive oil
1 garlic clove, crushed
250 g / 9 ounces lamb mince (ground lamb)
½ teaspoon salt
¼ teaspoon ground cumin
¼ teaspoon ground allspice
1 tablespoon chopped fresh flat-leaf parsley

TO FINISH
1 tablespoon dried mint
1½ teaspoons dried red pepper flakes
240 ml / 1 cup vegetable oil, for frying
120 g / ½ cup thick yoghurt (Greek yogurt)
2 garlic cloves, crushed
Salt
1 tablespoon toasted pine nuts

MAKES 20 TO 22 DUMPLINGS

To make the dough, combine the flour, a pinch of salt, and the olive oil in a bowl. Pour in the water slowly and knead the dough by hand for 2 to 3 minutes, until it's homogenous. Transfer the dough to a lightly floured work surface and continue kneading it for 5 to 10 minutes, until it's smooth.

Return the dough to a bowl, cover it with a cloth, and leave it to rest for about 30 minutes.

Meanwhile, make the filling. Heat the olive oil over medium-high heat. Add the garlic, lamb, salt, cumin, and allspice and sauté until the lamb is browned. Decrease the heat to medium and continue to cook for 5 to 6 minutes, until the lamb is cooked through.

Remove the pan from the heat and stir in the parsley.

To assemble the dumplings, cut the dough into four pieces. Flour a baking sheet and a work surface.

Working with one piece of dough at a time, roll out the dough to a thickness of 3 mm. Cut out circles about 2 cm / ¾ inch in diameter using a ravioli cutter, a cup, or a biscuit cutter. Put a spoonful of the filling in the middle of the circle, fold in half to make a half-circle, then pinch it around the edges to seal it. Bring the two ends together and pinch them to make a little hat-shaped dumpling. Place it on the floured sheet. Repeat with all the dough and filling, spacing out the dumplings so they don't stick together.

Bring a big pot of salted water to a boil over high heat. While the water heats, grease a baking sheet. Working in batches, boil the dumplings until they float, about 3 minutes. Scoop the dumplings out of the water with a spider or slotted spoon and transfer them to the greased sheet.

In a small ramekin, make a mix of the dried mint and red pepper flakes. One by one, dip the dumplings in the herbs to cover all the sides.

In a small frying pan, heat the vegetable oil to 180°C / 350°F.

Quickly fry the coated dumplings for a minute, using a spoon to turn them so they are fried on all sides. Drain on paper towels.

Combine the yoghurt and garlic with a pinch of salt in a bowl and mix well.

To serve, put a small circle of the garlic yoghurt on each plate. Place a few dumplings on the yoghurt and sprinkle the toasted pine nuts on top.

LENTIL SOUP WITH MAMA MICHELINE

There is no way to choose an absolute favourite from among all the delicacies that my mother has cooked for me throughout my life. She has a fantastic range—naturally most are Palestinian dishes, but she excels at some foreign ones, too. My parents would often entertain guests when I was growing up, and I would hear French, English, and Arabic spoken around the overflowing dining table. I liked the way that traditional Palestinian foods, such as koussa mahshi—stuffed courgettes (zucchini), kibbeh (spiced ground meat coated with bulgur wheat and fried), or shish barak (meat dumplings)—were served next to international ones, such as my maternal grandmother's sweet glazed carrots.

Like my brother and sister, I grew up munching on Mama's succulent mahshi—stuffed vegetables, rolled grape leaves, and rolled cabbage. She excels in making these to such an extent that when Jamie Oliver visited Palestine and wanted to learn how to make vegetarian versions, I had no choice but to hand him over to Mama Micheline.

A mild shrimp curry remains a trademark dish of my mother's. She learned how to make it from her mother-in-law, Emily, who also happened to be her aunt, and had been influenced and inspired by Indian cuisine while living in Bombay. In my opinion, my mother also makes the juiciest barbecued fillet of beef that I have ever tasted anywhere. But then there is her humble lentil soup, which makes me salivate just thinking of it. It is warm and comforting and quintessentially tastes of home.

A spoonful of Mama's lentil soup is creamy with a kick of ginger. It is perfect with a drop of freshly squeezed lemon and her crispy croutons. The combination creates a fabulous fragrance and texture. The soup is commonly made and served in winter. Coming home from school on a chilly day, I used to relish a bowl with spinach pastries on the side. To the outrage of my mother, I liked to dip the pastries into the lentil soup, enjoying the contrasting flavours.

The apparent simplicity of the soup is deceptive, as proven by the fact that I have never been able to perfect it or lay my hands on Mama's definitive recipe. If I ask her how to recreate it, she gives me a detailed account but only up to a point. She claims that each time she makes the soup, she changes the ingredients slightly. This may be true, but I suspect that she confuses me on purpose to keep the recipe secret and me in my place.

When I first opened my restaurant Fawda in Bethlehem, I made my best attempt at cooking Mama's lentil soup. However it was never quite as good as hers. Sensing my frustration, she made a huge pot of the soup at home and had it delivered to me. This provides an idea of the relationship that my mother and I have around food. Usually, I ask for her recipes, and she asks laughingly whether I will deconstruct or twist them. In return, I always share my plans and my mother gives her opinions and advice.

My mother has greatly influenced my cooking both as an amateur and a professional. She is always nurturing me. To this day, whenever we are both in Bethlehem, I tend to call her early in the morning to talk about our day. When I am busy, she will always kindly ask, "What do you want me to cook for you?" She knows my favourite dishes as well as she knows me; after all, she shaped my palate with the love of a mother. This applied even when we were travelling overseas—usually on trips to Europe—and she would help me choose what to order. My mother has an appreciation of fine dining that she has passed on to me. From a very young age, I was privileged to be able to dine in some of the world's best restaurants.

However, we did sometimes end up in awful places to eat, too. It was our family's habit to rent a car, particularly while visiting France. My father would drive and, as the oldest child, I would sit in the passenger's seat with a map, giving directions as we went off exploring the countryside. Mama would be in the back with my siblings, poring over the Michelin Guide for our next food stop. The method was hit-or-miss, but it ensured that food memories were part of my recollections of all our travels.

We spent the majority of time in Paris, where Mama would take us to newly opened restaurants or traditional brasseries that she enjoyed. Through her I was exposed to so many different cuisines and flavours that later I felt encouraged to experiment with tastes and textures in order to reinterpret Palestinian classic dishes and come up with my own modern takes.

But still I come back to my mother's lentil soup—her delicious reworking of the traditional kind you find in Palestine. Like her chocolate mousse, much loved by our extended family, it's a dish I have been striving to make ever since I was a child, never getting it a hundred percent right. My mother's talent and unpretentious style is on full display in these dishes. They are reminders of what makes her an exceptional cook.

LENTIL SOUP

My mother cooks *shorbat adas*, a lentil soup, for us as soon as the wind gets chilly in Bethlehem, and often in the days of Lent. Widely regarded as the healthy option to many a fast and as a food of the less fortunate, shorbat adas is in reality the noblest of soups, with its rituals of fresh accompaniments: Palestinian finely chopped salad, radishes, spring onions, and fried bread.

380 g / 13 ounces red lentils
4 tablespoons extra-virgin olive oil
2 onions, finely chopped
3 garlic cloves, crushed
2 teaspoons ground turmeric
2 teaspoons ground cumin
1 teaspoon ground ginger
500 ml / 2⅛ cups chicken stock or water
Juice of 2 lemons
2 flatbreads, such as pita, kmaj, or shrak
Green Shatta (page 76)

SERVES 6

Combine the lentils with cold water to cover in a bowl.

In a large pot, heat 2 tablespoons of the olive oil over medium-high heat. Add the onions and sauté for 2 minutes. Add the garlic, turmeric, cumin, and ginger and continue to sauté until the onions become translucent, another 3 minutes.

Drain the lentils and add to the pot. Cover with the stock and decrease the heat to medium. Cover and cook for 20 minutes, until the lentils are soft.

Add the lemon juice and blend with a handheld blender until creamy.

In a small pan, heat the remaining 2 tablespoons olive oil over medium-high heat. Cut the bread into strips and briefly fry in the hot oil, until lightly browned and crisp.

Serve the soup with fried bread on top and a dash of shatta.

MAFTOUL SALAD

2 tablespoons extra-virgin
    olive oil
1 onion, very finely
    chopped
250 g / 1½ cups maftoul
½ teaspoon salt
600 ml / 2½ cups water
¼ bunch flat-leaf parsley,
    leaves only
¼ bunch mint, leaves only
1 teaspoon dried marjoram
Juice of 1 lemon
150 g / ⅔ cup sun-dried
    tomatoes in oil
110 g / ⅓ cup cooked
    chickpeas, homemade
    or store-bought
2 tablespoons toasted
    almond slivers
1 teaspoon ground sumac

SERVES 6

Maftoul is a Palestinian delicacy, the hand-rolled maftoul grains symbolizing the attachment to wheat that we have in our culture. Palestinians still grow wheat despite the confiscation of land by the occupation forces. Maftoul is a celebratory dish that is usually prepared with chicken or meat and chickpeas. It is made for large family gatherings. However, it's also a fantastic grain for salads. I think maftoul is one of my favorite ingredients. The salad here is very simple, flavorful, and fresh; it reflects a lot of Palestine's flavours. In Bethlehem, it is called marma'on, and that name has survived in Bethlehem and in faraway places like Chile, where there are many Chileans of Palestinian origin, originally from Bethlehem, who have preserved the dishes and their names while adapting the recipes.

In a large pot, heat 1 tablespoon of the olive oil over medium-high heat. Add the onion and sauté until translucent, 3 to 5 minutes. Add the maftoul and stir until all the grains are well coated. Add the salt and water and simmer, uncovered, for about 15 minutes, until the maftoul has absorbed all of the water and is tender.

Remove the pot from the heat, cover, and set aside for 10 minutes. Then transfer onto a tray and fluff the maftoul with a fork, spreading it out so it cools down.

In the meantime, make the dressing. Put half the parsley and half the mint in a blender with the marjoram, the remaining 1 tablespoon olive oil, and the lemon juice and process until smooth.

Coarsely chop the remaining parsley and mint, slice the sun-dried tomatoes into thin strips, and, with your hand, separate the chickpeas into halves.

Plate the maftoul, drizzle the dressing over, and add the sun-dried tomatoes, chopped parsley and mint, and chickpeas. Sprinkle the almonds and sumac on top, and serve.

SILEK
SALAD

Silek is chard (also called silverbeet), a green that you will find grown and eaten all over Palestine, and cooked in many different ways. In Gaza, it is used to make sumaqqiyeh, a stew with silek, sumac, and red tahinia. Many Palestinian cooks stuff it like grape leaves. Here it makes a healthy, vibrant green, and tasty salad that is a staple on every dining table when silek is in season. In its simplicity, it celebrates the land and our extra-virgin olive oil.

3 tablespoons extra-virgin olive oil

1 onion, finely chopped

3 garlic cloves, crushed

2 bunches of silek (chard), stalks and leaves separated and finely chopped

½ teaspoon coarse sea salt

Juice of 1 lemon

½ teaspoon ground sumac

Heat the oil in a large pot over medium heat. Add the onion and garlic and sauté until softened, about 5 minutes. Add the silek stalks and sauté for 2 to 3 minutes, until softened. Add the leaves, stir well, add the salt, and sauté for another 2 to 3 minutes, until the stalks are golden and the leaves are wilted but still green. Decrease the heat, stir, and cook for another 10 to 12 minutes, until the leaves are tender.

Remove from the heat. Add the lemon juice and sumac and serve in a salad bowl, either warm or cold.

SERVES 4

OLIVE OIL WITH ABU MOHAMMAD IN SEBASTIA

Sebastia is a tiny hilltop village in the northern West Bank. Dating back to the Iron Age, it is thought to be one of the oldest continuously inhabited places in Palestine. All of the civilisations that took over this region settled in Sebastia. For a time, I would come as a tour guide, recounting for tourists how Salome was said to have danced here for Herod Antipas and then asked for the head of John the Baptist on a platter. We would look around what is believed to be the tomb of St. John—in the remnants of a Crusader church at one end of the Nabi Yahya Mosque. But the antiquities are not the main reason I keep returning to Sebastia. I come back to see my dear friend Abu Mohammad, and for his delicious food and the olive oil.

I met Abu Mohammad, a restaurant owner, on one of my first visits to Sebastia. He is known locally for his fantastic musakhan, an emblematic dish of Palestine, sometimes called our national dish. It is created with a dark taboun bread and soft onion confit coated in purple sumac and glistening olive oil, all crowned with roasted chicken. As well as being a formidable cook, Abu Mohammad is an impressive character who embodies the steadfast spirit of his village, the generosity and hospitality of Palestine, and its openness towards the world. Before Israel's occupation forces shut down the roads leading to Sebastia during the Second Intifada, his restaurant was constantly busy, welcoming pilgrims and travellers crossing from north to south. Even after the routes were reopened, business has never quite returned to how it was.

Whenever I plan to visit Sebastia or the bustling nearby city of Nablus, I am always wary of telling Abu Mohammad. There is no such thing as a snack with him, nor even a meal, only a feast. He will invite me and any guests I bring to meet him to have musakhan, but he always includes other dishes, too, knowing each is a favourite of mine and that I will find it impossible to resist. He will often start with a humble, earthy freekeh soup before adding a makloubeh, the

classic upside-down rice dish that includes slow-cooked cubes of lamb with aubergine (eggplant) or cauliflower—whichever is in season. Then there might be a stuffed lamb leg with the musakhan (roast chicken) served in the middle. Just when we are congratulating ourselves for devouring such a huge banquet, Abu Mohammad will smile and produce an irresistible tray of warm, sweet Nabulsi knafeh, a dessert with a shredded filo dough crust and a sweet cheese filling, topped with a rose water syrup.

Knowing Abu Mohammad as I do, I always take my stroll around Sebastia after greeting him but before sitting down at his overflowing table. Walking along the stones of ancient roads and among the crumbling walls and broken pillars poking through the green grass, I feel transported back through centuries. For me, the scenery represents the resilience of nature through past invasions and conflicts. There are olive trees spread among the ruins, or more accurately there are ruins spread among the olive trees. Some of these Palestinian trees date back to Roman times. They have stood as witnesses to so much change. Yet they represent constancy, too—the annual cycle of growth and harvesting that has instilled itself into Palestinian traditions and cuisine.

Olive oil is a staple in Palestine, but there are variations in how we use it. In the south of Palestine, we tend to use samneh (ghee) and olive oil separately and differently from in the northern West Bank. In the north, there is more agricultural land available for the production of olive oil, and there are fewer Bedouin who traditionally produce the sheep milk used to make samneh. Abu Mohammad, like other Palestinians from around Nablus and Jenin, will use olive oil routinely in cooking. He will fry eggs, dough, or cauliflower in olive oil.

A few years ago, I was filming an episode of my show, *Teta's Kitchen*, in Sebastia during the olive harvest season, which is always a joyful celebration. At the olive press, I had the pleasure of tasting the freshly pressed oil, which has a particular sharpness and spiciness to it that lessens with time. There is such pride and a sense of achievement as families arrive at the press after days of laborious teamwork picking these tiny fruits, grown on their trees on their land, as they have been for generations. At the press, I was touched by the kind gift of a bottle of freshly pressed olive oil by the woman who bakes the delicious taboun bread used locally for musakhan. She had a sparkle in her eyes.

I must have been caught up in the excitement of the olive harvest because I do not think Abu Mohammad had ever seen anybody use as much oil as I did that day when we were making musakhan together on camera. Instead of pouring the oil onto the edges of the bread and sprinkling it over the rest—which is soaked in chicken broth—I dipped the whole loaf into the oil, saturating it. It seems Abu Mohammad was easily converted to the process, however, as months later, when I was invited over for musakhan, I was surprised to see that he had begun dunking the bread into the oil, too.

The olive tree is often used as a symbol of Palestinian resilience and our connection to the land, and olive oil is tied up with our national identity. Over hundreds of years, a national tradition has built up around the harvest, with each village and city hosting its own festival at harvest time, often with *dabke* dancing and stalls selling local produce. Of course, there is also fierce competition among Palestinians over olive oil production. While we may accept that certain places are famous for different produce—for example, Beit Jala is known for its mishmish (apricots), and ennab, or jujube fruits, grow well in Ennab village near Sebastia—we vigorously dispute the source of the finest olive oil.

With Abu Mohammad, I've enjoyed our ongoing banter about whether olive oil from Bethlehem or Sebastia is the best. However, after years of arguing, I've decided to give up and just enjoy tasting and comparing the amazing olive oil from different places across the country whenever I get the chance.

FUKHARA POT ROAST

400 g / 14 ounces pork
   shoulder, cut into four
   equal pieces
400 g / 14 ounces beef
   shoulder, cut into four
   equal pieces
400 g / 14 ounces lamb
   shoulder, cut into four
   equal pieces
200 g / 7 ounces onions
4 garlic cloves
2 bay leaves
3 tablespoons coarse
   sea salt
6 sprigs parsley
3 sprigs zaatar (or
   substitute 1 tablespoon
   dry zaatar leaves)
60 ml / ¼ cup extra-virgin
   olive oil
40 g / ⅓ cup toasted
   pine nuts
40 g / ⅓ cup toasted
   almonds
About 200 ml / ¾ cup
   plus 2 tablespoons
   water, or more as
   needed

DOUGH SEAL
400 g / 3⅓ cups all-
   purpose flour, plus
   more for the work
   surface
5 to 6 teaspoons water
Salt and ground black
   pepper

SERVES 4

The *fukhara* is a clay pot that is used in Palestinian cuisine. It is traditionally filled with chicken or meat and vegetables and baked for hours in a wood-fired oven. I personally find that the vegetables lose their taste after a slow cook with meat in a sealed pot; therefore, I started experimenting with cooking the meat and the vegetables separately. I tried out different meats available in the Palestinian market until I came up with this delicious recipe.

Preheat the oven to 180°C / 350°F.

In a large bowl, mix together the meats, onions, garlic, bay leaves, coarse salt, parsley, zaatar, olive oil, pine nuts, and almonds. Transfer the mixture to a food-grade clay pot or a Dutch oven. Add the water to cover most of the meat.

To make the dough seal, mix the flour and the water until you have a dough. On a floured work surface, roll out the dough to make rope and place it on the inside edge of the cooking pot. Then place the cover on the pot.

Bake for 3½ hours. Break the dough seal to check if the meat is cooked and tender.

Strain the cooking juices into a small pot and place it over medium-high heat. Boil, checking constantly, until the juice thickens. Add salt and pepper to taste.

To serve, place a piece of each of the three meats in each bowl along with some cooked vegetables of your choice, and drizzle the juices on top.

BETHLEHEM

ROASTED BONE MARROW

Bone marrow isn't traditionally served on its own in Palestinian cuisine. However, many of our recipes—from mansaf to makloubeh to roasted lamb—involve cooking the meat with the bone. As a child, my grandmother used to always give me the bone marrow when cooking some of these dishes. In Arabic we call it *mokh* which means "brain." As child I assumed it was called that because it was good for the brain. But I loved the texture and appreciated how, depending on the way the meat was cooked, the texture of the bone marrow would be different. Much later in life, while in France, I started enjoying roasted beef bones with bone marrow, and I realised that I had been initiated into the secret of bone marrow very young. Here is a very simple roasted bone marrow recipe with a Palestinian twist.

1.3 kg / 2¾ pounds beef marrow bones, cut lengthwise
30 g / ¾ cup fresh zaatar leaves
15 g / ⅓ cup flat-leaf parsley leaves
1 teaspoon coarse sea salt
1 teaspoon cracked black pepper
½ teaspoon ground sumac
¼ teaspoon coriander seeds
1 teaspoon fresh lemon juice
1 garlic clove, crushed
Ka'ek al-quds (see page 72) or toasted pita bread

SERVES 6

Preheat the oven to 220°C / 425°F.

Place the bones marrow-side up on a baking sheet and roast for about 20 minutes, until the bone marrow starts bubbling.

Meanwhile, reserve a few leaves of zaatar and parsley for a garnish. In a mixing bowl, combine the rest of the zaatar and parsley with the salt, pepper, sumac, coriander seeds, lemon juice, and garlic. Whisk vigorously to combine.

When the bones are ready, drizzle the fragrant herb mix on the tops and on the sides and serve with the bread on the side.

QUINCE JAM

Quince, or *safarjal*, jam is another one of my childhood favorites. My grandmother used to make it, and nowadays my mother and I make it, too. It is a seasonal jam that I prepare and serve for guests at our boutique guesthouse, Hosh Al-Syrian, for a generous breakfast. Quince is an underappreciated fruit. It reminds me of Palestinian winters with its beautiful pinkish colour.

500 g / 2½ cups sugar
230 ml / 1 cup water
1 kg / 2⅛ pounds quince
10 g / 7½ teaspoons
    ground mastic
2 lemons, 1 chopped and
    1 juiced

MAKES FIVE 250 ML / 1-CUP JARS

Sterilize the canning jars. Place a plate in the freezer for checking the consistency of the jam. Have ready a piece of muslin or cheesecloth.

Fill the bottom of a double boiler with water and place over high heat. In the top of the double boiler, mix the sugar and water and bring to a boil. Decrease the heat to medium-high and cook for about 10 minutes until it forms a syrup.

Core the centers of the quince but don't peel them. Place the quince seeds and cores, mastic, and chopped lemon on the muslin. Tie the ends of the muslin to form a bag and slide it into the sugar syrup. Add the lemon juice.

Decrease the heat to low. Chop the quince and add to the syrup. Make sure you add the quince pieces immediately after chopping; otherwise they will oxidize and turn brown.

Increase the heat to medium and allow the quince to boil for 20 to 30 minutes, while stirring with a wooden spoon, until the jam thickens. Put a spoonful of the jam on the chilled plate to check the consistency. If you can pass a spoon in the middle of the jam and it leaves a mark, the jam is done. However, if it is still liquid and slides around, then you have to boil it for longer.

Once the jam is ready, pour it into the jars, seal, and leave them in a corner of the kitchen until they cool down. Enjoy quince jam for the rest of the year!

POACHED PEACHES IN POME-GRANATE JUICE

Peaches have a quite short season in Palestine. They're flavorful, and I think they go very well with a lot of desserts, including mouhalabieh (page 117). These peaches are poached in pomegranate juice flavoured with lavender. I usually pick the lavender and pomegranates from my garden, and I get local peaches from Um Nabil (see page 26).

In a saucepan, combine the sugar, water, and pomegranate juice over low heat and stir for 3 to 4 minutes until the sugar dissolves.

Turn the heat to high to let the mixture boil, and then decrease the heat to medium and add the lavender flowers.

With the tip of a knife, score an X at the base of each peach. Add the peaches to the saucepan, cover, and leave to cook for 8 minutes, or until the peaches are tender but still firm.

Meanwhile, prepare an ice bath with a bowl of water and ice cubes. With a spider or slotted spoon, remove the peaches from the syrup and immediately put them in the ice bath. Take them out of the bath and leave them in a sieve to drain. You can either remove the skin of the peaches (they should slip off easily) or keep them on. Store the peaches in the fridge while you finish the dish.

Place the saucepan with the syrup over medium-high heat and let it boil for 8 to 10 minutes, until it forms a very thick syrup.

Pour the syrup over the peaches and store in the fridge, but serve them soon; otherwise they will become mushy. Serve the peaches and fragrant syrup plain or alongside another dessert.

300 g / 1½ cups sugar
360 ml / 1½ cups water
175 ml / ¾ cup
    pomegranate juice
5 lavender flowers (the
    tips of the lavender
    sprigs)
6 ripe peaches

SERVES 6

GRAND LUNCHES WITH SIDO NAKHLEH

So many of our memories are intertwined with food. There are evocative tastes and smells, but the reminders of past meals and gatherings are also conjured by the plates, cutlery, furniture, and spaces we use. Most importantly, of course, there are the family and friends who created the dishes and brought us together.

My paternal grandfather, Nakhleh, loved good food and enjoyed nothing more than entertaining us with a grand family lunch. I am now privileged to live in his home and can easily transport myself back to the old days, when my grandfather, his sister Maria, his niece Victoria and cousin Regina would prepare to receive their guests. They would set out the silver cutlery that I continue to use, on the same wooden dining table, in the same *liwan*, or long, narrow central room. My grandfather was a tall gentleman whose gait I am reliably informed I have inherited by those who remember him strolling around Bethlehem's Old City. He was gentle and generous and loved to serve up stories of his childhood and global travels with each dish as he sat at the head of the table. Maria, Victoria, and Regina were in their seventies and eighties, and were typical Bethlehemites. Despite the fact that all three wore a solemn black as a kind of dress code, they were all remarkably fun.

A meal with Sido Nakhleh was always a feast of regal proportions. Always a food lover, I cherished these occasions. One Palestinian delicacy that we might be invited over to enjoy was stuffed lamb's intestines and tripe—the stomach lining. No longer so popular today, the offal would be well cleaned, cut into pieces, and stuffed with rice, meat, and chickpeas, then cooked in a yoghurt sauce. Rolled grape leaves filled with rice would be served on the side. I relished every mouthful.

There was also the excitement of variation and the unexpected with Sido Nakhleh. The cuisine at his home reflected the many regions that he and other relatives had visited and resided in over the years. My grandparents lived in

Japan and India, where my father was born, giving him a lifelong love of curry. There were also influences from places where Sido's brothers and sisters had moved to: Chile, Sudan, the UK, and Italy. Popular lunch dishes might include a mouthwatering spinach cannelloni or an escalope milanaise.

Once we arrived, Sido Nakhleh would guide us children toward the dining table. Even in his later years, when he was in a wheelchair, he remained an exemplary host, a soft and gentle presence. There was the joy of sharing exquisite tastes but also absorbing the side conversations sparked by the food or revolving around our daily lives.

Sido loved to expose us to exotic flavours, so if he could find a cherimoya— custard apple—he would cut it open and serve us each a small piece to sample with a spoon. My favourite fruit as a child was mango. Its appearance in season was made extra special by the fact that it would mark the only time when my grandfather would allow us to make a mess. I remember his expert lessons on how to slice the sweet flesh and remove the large seed. However, it was generally agreed that the best way to avoid wasting any of the delicious pulp was to use your hands and suck it from the seed. This would always leave us all chuckling and terribly sticky.

Dessert, whatever it might be, was always followed by Arabic coffee in the liwan and more of Sido's tales of past trips and exciting experiences.

Of all the children I was the only one allowed in Sido's pantry, which I later turned, perhaps appropriately enough, into my study. This is where the annual supplies were stored in the dark, away from the damaging effects of sunlight. For me, it was like a treasure trove: filled with jams, olive oil, dried molokhia (jute leaves), tomatoes, and pickled olives. Preserving fruits and vegetables when they were in season ensured that they could remain wondrously available to us all year round. The smell has faded now, but when I was a boy this room had the distinctive smell of molokhia.

Despite the availability of frozen molokhia in the market today, I still insist on drying molokhia leaves during the summer and storing it dried, just as it was dried and stored in my grandfather's pantry. I believe the taste is completely different. As with many other people in the Arab world, the dish is a childhood favourite that has stuck with me.

After my grandmother died, Sido's sister, niece, and cousin took care of the grocery shopping and preparing our feasts for the most part. However, a neighbour, a fantastic woman called Khadra, would sometimes come to help out. Originally from a Bedouin tribe just outside Bethlehem, Khadra had a striking look with a tattooed forehead and chin. At the time, these facial tattoos were common. But they have since disappeared in Palestine just like dried molokhia.

Nowadays, years after my grandfather and his household have left us, there are so many questions I would like to ask them. Having read through some of the neatly filed documents in the Kattan family archive, I can appreciate far more what courage Sido Nakhleh and his brothers had, travelling the world to seek their fortunes in the early twentieth century, towards the end of the Ottoman era. The name, Kattan, is Arabic for "cotton", and they ventured out to establish their trade in textiles. However, from this branch of my family only Sido Nakhleh and my grandmother, Emily, were to return to Palestine, in 1954.

They came back to dramatic change as a result of the 1948 Nakba (catastrophe), which saw more than 750,000 Palestinians displaced from their homes by the creation of the state of Israel, and the resulting violence and war. While the family home in Bethlehem remained safe, there were huge losses in investments and properties. The Nakba ensured that most family members who had already settled overseas did not return. Through his letters and stories, I can appreciate how much nostalgia my grandfather had for his early life with his siblings. There was also the terrible hole left by the early death of his wife.

The archive has many handwritten letters by Sido Nakhleh to my grandmother, Teta Emily, or El-Mimi, as he called her. The love they had for each other was something precious as they set out on international adventures and then came home to Bethlehem to face struggles and hardship. It impresses me more as an adult to remember how even in his final years, my grandfather remained an optimistic and cheerful person.

Yet he must always have wondered if events could have turned out differently. One poignant keepsake from my grandfather is a beautiful postcard of Bombay from 1947. He and my grandmother were evidently out celebrating on the night of India's independence. On the back of the postcard there are messages written by friends who were with them, expressing their wishes and hopes for the independence of Palestine as well.

CAULIFLOWER MAKLOUBEH

Makloubeh is one of the national dishes of Palestine. Each home, family, and region make makloubeh differently. But traditionally, there are two types: aubergine (eggplant) makloubeh with lamb, and cauliflower makloubeh with chicken. Both types are equally delicious, although at home, we tend to make aubergine makloubeh, as my father passionately dislikes cauliflower. Makloubeh translates to "upside down". The story goes that the name was created by Salah al-Din Yusuf ibn Ayyub, the former Sultan of Egypt. While visiting Palestine, a dish was served to him by flipping the pot upside down onto a tray. Not knowing its actual name, he used the term *makloubeh* to describe it, and that is how it has been known ever since.

CHICKEN
2 teaspoons ground allspice
1 teaspoon ground turmeric
1 teaspoon ground coriander
½ teaspoon ground cinnamon
2 teaspoons salt
1 teaspoon ground black pepper
1 whole chicken, about 1¾ kg / 4 pounds
2 tablespoons extra-virgin olive oil
1 onion, halved
2 bay leaves

CAULIFLOWER
300 ml / 1¼ cups vegetable oil
1 large cauliflower, cut into florets

RICE
720 g / 4 cups basmati rice
1 teaspoon ground allspice
½ teaspoon ground coriander
¼ teaspoon ground turmeric
¼ teaspoon ground cinnamon
1 tablespoon olive oil
2 tomatoes, sliced
2 onions, sliced
Water, as needed

GARNISH (OPTIONAL)
2 tablespoons whole almonds
2 tablespoons pine nuts

SERVES 6 TO 8

To prepare the chicken, combine the allspice, turmeric, coriander, cinnamon, salt, and pepper. Rub the mix into the chicken.

In a pot large enough to fit the whole chicken, heat the olive oil over medium-high heat. Add the onion and sear. Add the chicken, water to cover, and the bay leaves. When the water comes to a boil, decrease the heat to medium-low and simmer for 45 to 60 minutes, until the chicken is cooked through.

To prepare the cauliflower, fill a deep frying pan with the vegetable oil and heat it over medium-high heat to 180°C / 350°F. Working in batches, fry the cauliflower florets until they're golden, 2 to 3 minutes. Remove them from the oil with a spider or slotted spoon and drain them on paper towels.

Remove the chicken from the broth. Strain the broth through a sieve into a bowl. Add salt and pepper to taste. Cut the chicken into eight pieces.

To prepare the rice, rinse the rice in cold water until the water runs clear. Drain, place in a bowl, and add the spices to it, mixing well to coat the rice grains.

Pour the olive oil into a large pot. Layer the sliced tomatoes and onions in the bottom. Layer the chicken pieces on top with the skin-side down. Next add the fried cauliflower in a layer, then add the spiced rice. Pour in the strained broth until the rice is covered. If the broth does not cover the rice, add water and cover the pot.

Bring the broth to a boil, then decrease the heat to medium-low and simmer for about 45 minutes, until the rice is cooked. Turn off the heat and allow the steam to finish the cooking, about 10 minutes.

Meanwhile, to prepare the garnish if using, toast the almonds in a frying pan over medium heat for about 3 minutes. Add the pine nuts and toast for another minute, stirring. Do not allow the nuts to burn.

To serve, remove the pot lid. Cover the pot with a large serving tray and flip it upside down. Tap the bottom of the pot with your hands and leave it to sit for 5 minutes to make sure that the makloubeh has slipped off the pot onto the tray. Lift the pot; you should have a perfectly round makloubeh. If garnishing, sprinkle the toasted almonds and pine nuts on top before serving.

THE PERFECT GRILLED TRIO

In Palestinian culture, we often enjoy a barbecue. On weekends and evenings, driving through villages and towns, we are greeted by the smells of grilled meats and vegetables. When Palestinian families go out to eat, it is rarely for home-style food. Instead, it is for *mashwi*—grilled meats—and each area has its well-known eateries that also offer a variety of salads. They can be small hole-in-the-wall-type places or large established restaurants. My preferred grilled trio includes chicken kababs, lamb chops, and lamb kababs. Some people will argue the trio should include diced lamb or different cuts of chicken. However, these are my core favorites.

For all the kabobs, I prefer using metal skewers, but if you are using wooden ones, be sure to soak them in water for about 30 minutes before using.

CHICKEN KABABS
2 onions, finely chopped
5 garlic cloves, finely chopped
20 g / ½ cup fresh flat-leaf parsley, finely chopped
20 g / ½ cup fresh zaatar leaves, finely chopped
225 g / 1 cup yoghurt
60 ml / ¼ cup fresh lemon juice
60 ml / ¼ cup vegetable oil
1 teaspoon salt
½ teaspoon ground black pepper
¼ teaspoon ground cardamom
¼ teaspoon ground cinnamon
¼ teaspoon ground allspice
1 kg / 2¼ pounds boneless, skinless chicken breasts, cut into bite-size cubes

LAMB CHOPS
4 garlic cloves, very finely chopped
120 ml / ½ cup extra-virgin olive oil
1 tablespoon fresh lemon juice
1 tablespoon ground black pepper
2 teaspoons ground sumac
1 teaspoon ground cumin
1 teaspoon ground coriander
½ teaspoon ground cardamom
½ teaspoon ground cinnamon
½ teaspoon ground nutmeg
Salt
12 bone-in lamb rib chops

LAMB KABABS
750 g / 1⅔ pounds lamb mince (ground lamb)
1 onion, finely chopped
2 garlic cloves, finely chopped
1 parsley sprig, finely chopped
1 teaspoon ground allspice
½ teaspoon ground nutmeg
½ teaspoon ground cardamom
½ teaspoon ground cumin
Salt and ground black pepper

SERVES 6

CONTINUED ON NEXT PAGE

To prepare the chicken kababs, combine the onions, garlic, parsley, zaatar, yoghurt, lemon juice, vegetable oil, salt, pepper, cardamom, cinnamon, and allspice in a bowl. Add the chicken and mix until the chicken is fully coated. Cover and marinate in the refrigerator for 4 to 8 hours. Thread the chicken onto skewers, leaving the tops and the bottoms of the skewers empty to place them on the barbecue.

To prepare the lamb chops, combine the garlic, olive oil, lemon juice, pepper, sumac, cumin, coriander, cardamom, cinnamon, and nutmeg in a large bowl. Season with salt and mix together. Add the lamb chops, toss until well-coated, cover the bowl, and marinate in the refrigerator for 3 hours.

To prepare the lamb kababs, combine the lamb mince in a bowl with the onion, garlic, parsley, allspice, nutmeg, cardamom, and cumin. Season with salt and pepper. Use your hands to mix until everything is evenly combined. In the palm of your hand, form the meat into oval patties about 4 cm / 1½ inches thick. Thread the patties onto skewers, leaving the tops and the bottoms of the skewers empty to place them on the barbecue. Refrigerate while you prepare the rest of the meal.

Prepare your charcoal or gas barbecue for medium-high heat on one side and lower heat on the other side, as we will sear the meats over high heat and then let them cook through on the other side.

Start with the chicken skewers. Place them over the hotter side of the barbecue first. Cook for 5 minutes on each side, for a total of 10 minutes. Move them to the lower-heat side of the barbecue and leave them over low heat for another 1 to 2 minutes to cook completely.

Place the lamb chops over the hotter side for about 3 minutes on each side for medium-rare cooking. It's possible to leave them for an extra minute over low heat if you prefer them cooked more. Allow them to rest before serving.

Place the lamb kababs over the hotter side for 4 minutes on each side, for a total of 8 minutes. Then move them to the lower-heat side of the barbecue and leave them over low heat for 1 to 2 minutes, depending on the level of doneness you prefer for the meat. *Sahtain*!

MUSAKHAN-INSPIRED CHICKEN LIVER PÂTÉ

This was maybe my first experimental take on musakhan, as I tried to get inspiration from a very traditional Palestinian dish. And from that traditional dish, it became a chicken liver pâté, a cold dish. I twisted the textures of the components, but it still has olive oil, chicken, sumac, onions, and taboun bread. I think it is a great recipe that you can play around with and make into bite-size or more substantial portions to be served as a starter around a beautiful table of other Palestinian dishes.

PÂTÉ
60 ml / ¼ cup extra-virgin olive oil
300 g / 10 ounces chicken liver
60 g / ¼ cup unsalted butter
½ teaspoon salt
½ teaspoon ground sumac
¼ teaspoon freshly ground black pepper
2 tablespoons fresh lemon juice

ONION JAM
60 ml / ¼ cup extra-virgin olive oil, plus more to sprinkle
3 large onions, diced
100 g / ½ cup sugar
1 tablespoon ground sumac, plus more to sprinkle
90 ml / ¾ cup white balsamic vinegar
1 pinch of salt

TO FINISH
Taboun bread
Ground sumac
Olive oil

SERVES 6

To make the pâté, in a large frying pan, heat the olive oil over medium-high heat. Add the liver and sauté until cooked through and golden on the outside, 3 to 5 minutes. Scrape into the bowl of a food processor, leaving the oil in the pan. Add the butter, salt, sumac, pepper, and lemon juice. Whiz the ingredients until they are well blended.

Transfer the mixture to a sheet of parchment paper. Roll it into a log 4 cm / 1½ inches thick, and tie the parchment paper in several places to secure it. Roll it in cheesecloth and place in the fridge overnight.

To make the onion jam, heat the olive oil in a large pot over medium-high heat. Add the onions and sauté until they're practically golden brown, about 15 minutes. Decrease the heat, add the sugar and sumac, and leave to cook for 5 to 6 minutes, until the sugar has melted. Increase the heat to cook until the onion is caramelised, another 5 minutes. Decrease the heat to very low, add the vinegar, and stir the mixture until it has a jamlike consistency. Season with salt and let it cool. Once it's warm, transfer it to a glass jar. When the jam is at room temperature, seal the jar and keep it at room temperature until the pâté is ready.

To serve, place the bread on a serving plate. Slice the pâté and place it on top of the bread. Place a bit of onion jam on the side or on top, and then sprinkle a bit of sumac and a bit of olive oil on the plate.

THE BETHLEHEM ARAB WOMEN'S UNION

The Bethlehem Arab Women's Union (AWU) touches many aspects of my life. My grandmother, Julia Kattan Dabdoub, was one of the founders in 1947, when it was set up as a first aid centre for those who were forcibly displaced during the Nakba, the "catastrophe" that came with the creation of the state of Israel. By 1948, more than 700,000 Palestinians had lost their homes and land and ended up in the West Bank, Gaza, and neighbouring countries: Lebanon, Syria, and Jordan. My grandmother and her friends tried to provide small-scale help in our city in the midst of the misery.

Located in the Old City, over the years, the union continued its charitable work and soon became a cultural and social hub, too. It promoted progressive values and had the first public mixed-gender swimming pool, the first library, and the first art school in Bethlehem. It continues to run an ethnographic museum and also an embroidery project and a kitchen that preserves Palestinian traditions while helping local women find an income. To this day, it organises lunches for senior citizens and activities for vulnerable children.

The AWU was so central to my grandmother's daily life that growing up it was also part of mine. Of course, the food production was my favourite part. I loved to watch the different women coming together—some from old Bethlehemite families, others from the refugee community and from surrounding villages, their different backgrounds bringing different touches to the recipes. As I discovered when I filmed my show, *Teta's Kitchen*, there is no better way to spark a lively debate among Palestinians than by trying to discern the correct method to make a favourite dish.

Even now, the AWU makes delicious savoury pastries: spinach pies, or khobz bi sabanekh, which have a distinctive, slightly sour taste; sambousek which are semi-circular with thick crusts and filled with meat or cheese; and sfiha, round fluffy flatbreads filled with a spiced meat flavoured with tahinia. They also have an olive oil–based sweetbread called farayek which is topped with sesame seeds and often eaten during Lent when many Christians forgo dairy. This has a wonderful aroma, which fills the building. Very often my family and I still buy the different pastries fresh or frozen for party food and snacks.

Many of the activities of the AWU take place in its large central hall, and these introduced me to important Palestinian artistic and political figures. I remember being recruited on one occasion to help Teta Julia install an exhibition for the esteemed Palestinian artist and anthropologist Ali Qleibo. Another time, not long after what we believed at the time was a breakthrough Oslo peace agreement, the space was rented out by a politician named Salah Tamari, an icon of the Palestinian resistance. He had been freed from an Israeli jail during one of the first prisoner exchanges with the Palestinian Liberation Organisation. He then went on to further his education, get married to an ex-wife of Jordan's King Hussein, Princess Dina, and return to Palestine. He became governor of Bethlehem.

Every Thursday, Salah Tamari held open sessions for locals to share their grievances on a multitude of problems from power shortages to health care and infrastructure. He would invite heads of public service to help find solutions. The first time I watched one of these public sessions, when I was twenty years old, my cynicism must have shown through, as my grandmother teased me about it. But later, I got the chance to talk to the governor, taking a stroll around the building. We began talking about poetry and he began reciting T. S. Eliot's *The Waste Land*. I was fascinated and hugely impressed. I promptly told my grandmother that Mr. Tamari was a great man, and she laughed merrily at my turnaround. She said, "That is what the Arab Women's Union does, it tries to bring good people together and serve every citizen of the city."

If I want to feel close to my late grandmother or give a visitor a special insight into Bethlehem, then I always go to the small ethnographic museum that my grandmother was closely involved in setting up. It is just off Star Street, a short walk from Manger Square and the Nativity Church, but can be easily missed down a side passage. The museum, called Beituna al-Talhami, our Bethlehem Home, was founded in 1972. Two typical old houses have been taken over to give a taste of local living in the late nineteenth and early twentieth century. There is an impressive collection of black-and-white photographs and collections from people's homes—many donated. These include the traditional costumes—exquisitely handwoven thobes (ankle-length robes worn by women), headdresses, and tarboush (brimless hats like truncated cones)—intricate carpets, and fancy jewelry.

My favourite room of the museum is the kitchen, which has a collection of objects that I love to study. There were clearly evolutions over time, from pottery

تقدمة من ستوديو شامية

to tin and brass, before modern materials like Teflon ever came on the scene. We switched from wood fire to coal fires, to butane gas burners. At the same time, many aspects of our cuisine and our cooking methods remained steady. Staples such as olive oil, olives, jams, honey, and dibs (grape molasses) have clearly not changed. Then we have the same preservation techniques: how we dry our *bamia* (okra), grape leaves, molokhia (jute), garlic, and tomatoes, for example. There are some practices and devices that I would love to bring back, first among them the use of the *namliya* which takes its name from *namla*, or ant. This ingenious cube-shaped structure dangles down from a thin wire hung from the high-arched ceiling in the kitchen and has fine-metal mesh covering each side—including one with a door. Before the days of refrigerators, this was how we protected food from invading armies of insects.

Tracing the origin of dishes can be fascinating. Koussa mahshi and mahshi beitan jan—stuffed courgettes and aubergines (zucchini and eggplant)—are an ever-popular, emblematic Palestinian dish. In Bethlehem, they were often served for Sunday lunch in Christian households—they could be cored and stuffed with rice and meat, with grape leaves rolled a day before—then put in a pot over a low fire to cook while the family was at Mass. However, I remember when I was young enjoying an unfamiliar version at the house of our relatives Nasri and Margot Jacir. I soon realised that the vegetables had been dried and salted before being rehydrated. In the past, before greenhouses and refrigeration brought us these vegetables almost year round, this was how we preserved them to eat out of season. The method has now disappeared from our town, but I have tried a few times to recreate it—working on the texture and recipe.

At the AWU's Beituna al-Talhami museum, my head will always be filled with food thoughts and nostalgia as I mount the last flight of stairs to the final room at the top of the house: the bedroom. This is an homage to Bethlehem in the 1920s in particular, and a photograph of my grandmother, who donated so many of the items here, greets you. During this time period, for my family as well as for many other local ones, there was an interplay between Bethlehem, Europe, and the wider world. Some Bethlehemite businesses had offices in Kiev, Manila, Paris, London, Manchester, Santiago, and Barranquilla, Colombia. People from the town were getting good use out of their passports embossed with "Palestine, British Mandate".

This was a time of rapid change, represented in terms of people's clothes which became more influenced by Western fashions. The room has wonderful photos of the period: my grandmothers and all their sisters—one dressed as a nun—posing together, my grandmother as a child emerging from a wedding at the Nativity Church, and a small picture of both my grandmothers in a horse-drawn carriage in the orange groves of Tel Al-Rish, a suburb of Jaffa before 1948. For me, this part of the museum is full of references to my grandmother's book, *Lest We Forget*—lest we forget the culture, the food of Palestine, lest we forget our love of Bethlehem, our brothers and sisters in the diaspora, the complexity and enduring beauty of life here. As her little nod to me, there is a special piece of furniture I see as I leave this room: a wooden cradle. The last occupant of that small wooden bed was me.

LOUKMET BROCCOLI

450 g / 1 pound broccoli, cut into 3 cm / 1¼-inch florets
4 garlic cloves, peeled
1 teaspoon salt
1 teaspoon dill seeds
2 teaspoons chilli-infused olive oil (or substitute 2 teaspoons extra-virgin olive oil and ½ teaspoon red pepper flakes)
Juice of 1 lemon

SERVES 4

Broccoli, in its initial wild cabbage form, originated in the eastern Mediterranean region before travelling with the Romans to Italy and being "engineered" by the Etruscans onwards to create what you now find in northern Europe and the United States. Very often, seeing a stalk of broccoli poking out from a local market stall, I would wonder why this delicious vegetable did not make it into the traditional repertoire of Palestinian cuisine, until I understood that engineered broccoli as we know it today returned home to the eastern Mediterranean much later. Some spices and seeds are specific to regional cuisines in Palestine and one of them is dill seeds, *ein jarada*. Not found in the West Bank and coastal areas, it is widely used in Gaza.

Bring a large pot of salted water to a boil and prepare an ice bath.

Add the florets to the boiling water to blanch for 1 to 2 minutes, until bright green and tender-crisp. Remove from the boiling water and immediately submerge in the ice bath for about 5 minutes, until cool. Drain well.

In a mortar, crush the garlic and salt into a paste and then add half the dill seeds and continue crushing.

Add the olive oil and the lemon juice. In a rotating movement with the pestle, mix well into a dressing.

Serve the broccoli drizzled with the dressing and sprinkle the remaining dill seeds on top.

BETHLEHEM

FREEKEH SALAD

The charred green wheat, freekeh, has such a distinctive flavour. Smoky and evocative of the earth it stems from, it is a superb grain to cook with. Traditionally used in lieu of rice, freekeh has nourished generations of Palestinians since 2000 BC. This simple salad is one of many ways to celebrate freekeh.

90 ml / 6 tablespoons extra-virgin olive oil
200 g / 7 ounces cracked freekeh, rinsed and any stones removed
1 L/ 4¼ cups water
Salt
400 g / 14 ounces carrots with tops, carrots chopped, tops finely chopped
500 g / 1⅛ pounds spring greens, such as young cabbage, halved and thinly sliced
2 garlic cloves, crushed
2 tablespoons fresh lemon juice
2 spring onions (scallions), finely chopped
30 g / ¾ cup mint leaves, coarsely chopped
30 g / ⅔ cup parsley leaves, coarsely chopped
1 teaspoon ground sumac

SERVES 4

Heat 1 tablespoon of the oil in a saucepan over medium heat. Add the freekeh, sauté it for 30 seconds, then add the water and ½ teaspoon salt. Bring the water to a boil, reduce the heat to low, cover, and leave to cook for 15 minutes. Remove the saucepan from the heat, keep covered, and set aside for 20 minutes.

Uncover and let the freekeh cool until you are ready to assemble the salad.

Heat 1 tablespoon of the oil in a pan over medium heat. Add the chopped carrots and sauté until they are slightly charred, 7 to 8 minutes. Transfer to a bowl and set aside.

In the same pan, heat 1 tablespoon of the oil, add the spring greens and a sprinkle of salt, and cook until the greens are wilted, 2 to 3 minutes.

To make the dressing, in a small bowl, combine the garlic, remaining 3 tablespoons of olive oil, and the lemon juice. Mix well.

Fluff the cold freekeh with a fork. Add the spring onions, cooked carrots, wilted greens, and the chopped mint and parsley. Fold in the dressing. Transfer to a serving bowl, use the carrot tops as a garnish, and sprinkle the sumac on last.

WINTER

BETHLEHEM

QALAYET BANDOURA WITH POACHED EGGS

Qalayet bandoura is a reduced tomato stew that we have for breakfast, and sometimes people crack an egg on top of it and put it in the oven. Some also enjoy it as a side for fried eggs. Slow cooking adds a depth of flavour to the dish and brings out the flavours of the land of Palestine. The poached eggs on top break beautifully over the stew, creating an ideal texture. Some people blanch the tomatoes to remove the skin; I personally prefer keeping it on, but feel free to make it as you wish.

In a frying pan over medium-high heat, warm 1 tablespoon of the olive oil. Add the chillies and garlic and sauté for 1½ minutes, until they start releasing their flavors and scents. Chop the tomatoes and add to the pan. Add salt and pepper to taste and decrease the heat to medium-low. Cook for 20 to 25 minutes, until the tomatoes break down. Add a small amount of water if the tomatoes dry out.

Reduce the heat to low and cook for another 10 to 15 minutes, until the stew thickens. Add the remaining tablespoon of olive oil to the pan, stir, remove the pan from the heat, and cover. Divide the stew among four plates or serving bowls and keep it warm while preparing the poached eggs.

To poach the eggs, fill a large pot with boiling water and put it over high heat to maintain the boiling temperature. Crack the eggs one by one into a fine sieve over bowl to remove the more liquid part of the egg white. Put each egg into a small bowl.

Reduce the heat to low, add vinegar to the water, then stir to create a vortex in the middle.

Drop one egg into the vortex and leave to cook for 2½ to 3 minutes, depending on how runny you like your eggs. Remove the egg with a slotted spoon and place on top of a mound of stew. Repeat the process with the other eggs.

Sprinkle parsley on top of each serving and add a dash of olive oil and a sprinkle of sumac.

2 tablespoons extra-virgin olive oil, plus more to serve
1 red chilli, chopped
1 green or red chilli, chopped
2 garlic cloves, crushed
500 g / 18 ounces tomatoes
Coarse or kosher salt and ground black pepper
Water (optional)
2 tablespoons white vinegar
4 eggs
20 g / ½ cup chopped fresh flat-leaf parsley
Ground sumac

SERVES 4

FREEKEH RISOTTO

This recipe—a deeply earthy and creamy celebration of the smoky freekeh of the north of Palestine and the beauty of the baladi cheese—first saw the day at Fawda in Bethlehem, then became a classic at Akub in London.

Historically freekeh was the essential grain along with bulgur in Palestine, until rice appeared and slowly replaced it. Some classic dishes still retain freekeh as the base; other dishes are slowly replacing rice with freekeh, to capture that smoky fragrance.

1½ L / 6 cups vegetable broth
A few sage leaves
1 tablespoon saffron threads, crushed
4 tablespoons extra-virgin olive oil
2 small onions, minced
A pinch of ground cardamom
A pinch of ground ginger
320 g / 2 cups cracked freekeh, rinsed and any stones removed
240 ml / 1 cup crisp white wine (I use Palestinian Sauvignon Blanc)
130 g / ½ cup crumbled baladi cheese (or substitute feta cheese)
Coarse sea salt and freshly ground white pepper

SERVES 4 TO 6

Combine the vegetable broth, sage leaves, and the saffron threads in a pot over medium heat.

In a larger pot, heat 3 tablespoons of the olive oil. Add the onions and cook until soft, about 3 minutes. Stir in the cardamom and ginger. Add the freekeh and stir the mixture for 3 to 4 minutes. Add the wine and cook until the wine has evaporated.

Add 120 ml / ½ cup warm broth to the freekeh and stir until absorbed. Continue adding 120 ml / ½ cup broth in the same way, stirring until absorbed. When the freekeh is cooked and creamy, turn off the heat and stir in the remaining 1 tablespoon of olive oil, the cheese, and salt and white pepper to taste.

EJJEH (OMELETTE)

Ejjeh is the Palestinian omelette; it can be served plain or packed with ingredients. Sometimes I like to get a little creative. At Hosh Al-Syrian, we serve a standard ejjeh with tomato, onion, parsley, and often something extra, such as seasonal fresh herbs from the market.

12 eggs
60 ml / ¼ cup heavy cream
10 g / ¼ cup flat-leaf parsley leaves, finely chopped
10 g / ½ cup spinach, chopped
5 g / ¼ cup mint, chopped
2 tablespoons fresh or dried zaatar leaves
1 teaspoon salt
1 teaspoon ground black pepper
1 tablespoon all-purpose flour
4 tablespoons extra-virgin olive oil
1 small onion, finely chopped

SERVES 6

Crack the eggs into a big bowl. Add the cream and whisk until combined. Add half the parsley, half the spinach, half the mint, half the zaatar, and all the salt and pepper. Whisk in the flour until all the ingredients are well mixed.

In a frying pan, heat 2 tablespoons of the olive oil over medium heat. Add the onion and sauté briefly. Remove from the pan with a slotted spoon and combine with the remaining parsley, spinach, mint, and zaatar in a small bowl.

Into the same frying pan, pour 160 ml / ⅔ cup of the egg mixture into the middle of the pan. Swirl the pan around to make sure that the eggs spread to all sides. Let cook for 2 to 3 minutes, until the bottom is set. Sprinkle about one-sixth of the herb-and-onion mixture in the middle. Fold, then flip the omelette over and continue to cook for another 2 minutes. Transfer to a plate.

Repeat with the rest of the egg mixture, adding some of the remaining 2 tablespoons olive oil to the pan each time, until you have used all of it. You should end up with six omelettes.

KOFTA SANDWICHES

Kofta, shaped minced meat patties, is typically the first meat children eat in Palestine. It is cooked in tomato sauce and served with rice. It's an excellent comfort food, one that I think of whenever I need a quick and comforting home-cooked meal. Kofta sandwiches are also a treat on the side of a barbecue, or you can rustle one up as an evening snack. The advantage of this recipe is that you can make it either on a barbecue or in a pan.

KOFTA

600 g / 1¼ pounds beef mince (ground beef)
400 g / 14 ounces lamb mince (ground lamb)
1 onion, finely chopped
20 g / ½ cup flat-leaf parsley leaves, finely chopped
½ teaspoon ground black pepper
½ teaspoon ground coriander
½ teaspoon dried red pepper flakes
½ teaspoon ground allspice
¼ teaspoon salt
¼ teaspoon ground cinnamon
Olive oil, for brushing

TAHINIA SAUCE

140 g / ½ cup tahinia
Juice of 1 lemon
1 tablespoon extra-virgin olive oil
2 garlic cloves, crushed
½ teaspoon salt
120 ml / ½ cup water

SANDWICHES

4 kmaj (pita breads), halved
Fresh mint leaves
Sliced cucumber pickles
½ teaspoon Green Shatta (page 76)
1½ teaspoons extra-virgin olive oil

SERVES 4 TO 6

To make the kofta, line a baking sheet with parchment paper.

In a bowl, mix the beef, lamb, onion, parsley, pepper, coriander, red pepper flakes, allspice, salt, and cinnamon until well-blended. In the palm of your hand, form the meat into oval patties about 4 cm / 1½ inches thick. You should have around 20 patties. If you are grilling them, thread them onto metal skewers, leaving the tops and bottoms of the skewers empty to place them on the barbecue. Once they are shaped, place them on the prepared sheet and refrigerate for 30 minutes.

Meanwhile, if you are going to barbecue them, prepare a charcoal or gas barbecue for medium-high heat.

While the kofta chill, make the tahinia sauce. Combine the tahinia, lemon juice, olive oil, garlic, and salt in a blender and mix until well-blended. With the motor running, add the water slowly until the sauce is creamy and thick.

When you're ready to cook, brush the kofta with a bit of olive oil and place them on the barbecue or in a frying pan over medium-high heat. Cook them for 2 to 3 minutes per side. Keep turning them every 2 to 3 minutes for about 10 minutes, until cooked through.

To assemble the sandwiches, cut open the kmaj, add some of the tahinia sauce, the kofta, mint leaves, and pickles. Mix the shatta with olive oil to dilute it and drizzle on top. Enjoy!

BETHLEHEM

SQUASH CREAM SOUP WITH LABAN JAMEED

When temperatures drop, winter squash starts appearing all over Palestine. The squash have fantastic flavors as they benefit from the relatively mild winters of Palestine and absorb some of our sunshine so the taste has some sweetness to it. For this soup, I combine the umami of the laban jameed (salted and dried yoghurt) with the creamy, velvety texture of the roasted butternut squash and add a hint of zaatar.

2 tablespoons extra-virgin olive oil

1 butternut squash, about 1.5 kg / 3⅓ pounds halved lengthwise and seeded

1 tablespoon dried zaatar leaves

Salt

¼ teaspoon ground black pepper

¼ teaspoon ground nutmeg

1 small onion, finely chopped

3 garlic cloves, finely chopped

720 ml / 3 cups vegetable broth, plus more if needed

30 g / 1 ounce laban jameed (dried and salted yoghurt, see page 33)

½ bunch parsley, chopped

Olive oil

SERVES 6

Preheat the oven to 220°C / 425°F.

Drizzle 1 teaspoon of the olive oil on the flesh of each squash half and rub in well. Sprinkle the zaatar, 1 teaspoon salt, the pepper, and nutmeg evenly on both sides and rub in well. Place the squash on a baking sheet and roast for about 45 minutes, until the squash is soft, browned, and starting to caramelise.

In a large pot, heat the remaining 1 tablespoon plus 2 teaspoons olive oil over medium heat and add a sprinkle of salt. Add the onion and sauté for 4 to 5 minutes, or until the onion is coloured. Add the garlic and sauté for another minute.

To finish the soup with a handheld blender, scoop the inside of the butternut squash into the pot. Add the broth and process until the soup is creamy and smooth. Add more broth if you find it's necessary to get the right consistency.

Ladle the soup into bowls and garnish with the crumbled laban jameed, parsley, and a splash of olive oil.

ZNOUD EL SIT

These rich filo pastries are filled with qishta (a cream filling), fried, and soaked in an orange blossom syrup. Their name means "forearms of a lady", alluding to the shape of the pastry. This is an indulgent dessert served often either at the end of the meal or with a cup of Arabic coffee to visitors any time of the day.

SYRUP
200 g / 1 cup sugar
120 ml / ½ cup water
1 tablespoon fresh
   lemon juice
1 teaspoon orange
   blossom water
2 teaspoons rose water

QISHTA
500 ml / 2⅛ cups whole
   milk
500 ml / 2⅛ cups heavy
   cream
120 g / ¾ cup plus
   2 tablespoons cornflour
   (cornstarch)
100 g / ½ cup sugar
1 tablespoon rose water

PASTRY
15 to 20 filo pastry sheets,
   defrosted
120 g / ½ cup unsalted
   butter, melted
Vegetable oil, for frying
50 g / ⅓ cup pistachios,
   finely chopped
8 g / ¼ cup aromatic
   organic rose petals

MAKES 14 PASTRIES

To prepare the syrup, combine the sugar, water, and lemon juice in a pot over medium heat. Stir constantly until the consistency thickens, 10 to 12 minutes. Remove the pan from the heat, stir in the orange blossom water and the rose water, then set aside to cool.

To prepare the qishta, combine the milk, cream, cornflour, and sugar in a pot over medium heat. Whisk continuously, until everything dissolves and the qishta thickens, about 10 minutes. Remove from the heat, continue whisking, and add the rose water. Cover with plastic wrap, pressing directly on top so it doesn't form a skin. Cool in the fridge for 2 hours.

To assemble the pastries, take the stack of filo sheets and cut the stack into four strips, each 10 cm / 4 inches wide. Cut a single piece in half widthwise. Place on top of two stacked long filo strips, to form a cross.

Scoop 1½ tablespoons of the qishta on top of the filo, at the centre where the filo sheets meet. Fold the sides of the shorter strip over the qishta. Roll the longer strip around it, to form a cigar shape. Roll tightly but gently. Brush the formed log on all sides with melted butter and place them on a baking sheet. Continue until all the filling is used.

Heat 2½ cm / 1 inch of oil in a frying pan to 180°C / 350°F. Pour the syrup into a bowl and set it nearby.

Working in batches, fry the pastries on each side until crispy and golden, about 4 minutes total. With tongs, plunge the pastries into the syrup quickly and then arrange on a serving plate. Decorate with the pistachios and rose petals.

BURBARA

In Palestine, the first weeks of December are when Christmas starts poking its nose in. We celebrate Eid al-Burbara, the feast of Saint Barbara, with a sweet pudding that perfumes the first cold evenings of Bethlehem's winter.

180 g / 1 cup wheat berries
720 ml / 3 cups water, plus boiling water if needed
65 g / ⅓ cup sugar
2 cinnamon sticks
1 teaspoon ground anise
1 teaspoon ground fennel
140 g / 1 cup chopped mixed dried fruits (apricots, raisins, and so on)

TOPPINGS (OPTIONAL)
Walnuts, almonds, pine nuts, and/or pistachios
Pomegranate seeds
Fennel candy and/or candied chickpeas
Sugar-coated chickpeas and/or almonds

SERVES 6

Soak the wheat berries overnight in cold water to cover. Drain well.

Bring the 720 ml / 3 cups water to a boil in a pot over high heat. Decrease the heat to medium and add the wheat berries, sugar, and cinnamon sticks. Cook for 15 minutes, stirring regularly so the berries don't stick to the bottom of the pot. Add the anise, fennel, and dried fruits and cook for another 20 minutes, until the wheat berries are tender and fluffy. If all the water evaporates before the berries are tender, add up to 120 ml / ½ cup boiling water.

Serve in small bowls and decorate with any or all of the toppings.

CELEBRATING CHRISTMAS IN BETHLEHEM

Family gatherings for Christmas in Bethlehem always begin early in December with Burbara (page 205), a sweet, spiced wheat porridge–like dessert which I truly love, made in honour of Saint Barbara. Eid al-Burbara, or Saint Barbara's Day, is celebrated twice, as are many Christian holidays in Palestine: first on December 4 for Catholics and then on December 17, according to the older calendar used by the Greek Orthodox. Most extended Christian families like mine include members of different denominations.

The burbara frenzy begins at the spice shops where all the necessary ingredients are bought—the wheat, dried fruits and nuts, ground fennel and anise, and the candies often used as a decoration, along with bright red pomegranate seeds.

A joyous part of the ritual of burbara is that it is widely shared with helpings offered to neighbours and friends, regardless of their religious affiliations. Growing up, there were always invitations from different family members and friends we were close to throughout December. Different cooks prefer their own variations on the burbara recipe, and sampling these only enhanced the pleasure of the gatherings.

Eating burbara is also about sharing the intriguing tale of Saint Barbara. It is said that after Barbara converted to Christianity, her pagan father was enraged and ordered her to be captured, tortured, and beheaded. However, she hid in a wheat field where the crop grew to hide and protect her. These long-ago events are supposed to have happened in a Palestinian village north of Ramallah called Aboud.

Another tradition associated with the holiday is to grow shoots of wheat from seeds and use these to decorate the Christmas nativity crèche.

After the resplendent Christmas lunch that was always served at my grandparents' home, the evening of the 24th of December necessitated another

meal to see us through the late-night Mass. That would tend to be a combination of a French and Palestinian buffet. Basically whoever was residing in France at that time or had recently visited was obliged to return weighed down with the Christmas essentials—as many French cheeses and as much charcuterie as they could manage. Palestinian salads were also a must, as well as shawarma, ham, and cold roast cuts and plenty of pickles and breads. So long as there were small children among us, Santa Claus would visit. Then we would tuck into more of Teta Julia's delicious Christmas cake.

On the 25th itself, Christmas Day, it would fall to my parents to offer their magnificent spread to family and friends. My father delighted in orchestrating the drinks, paying special attention to the choices of wines, and the Christmas carols while my mother took care of the food. Turkey is not widely seen as a traditional Christmas lunch by Palestinians, but sometimes we would opt for a huge bird as the main course. Otherwise, there would be more roast lamb and often a generous ham, complementing my grandmother's choices from the day before, served with another festive rice dish.

Desserts came in many forms, my father having a taste for an English Christmas pudding and my Francophile mother responding with a bûche de Noël or perhaps her famous chocolate mousse. Then there would be a tray of syrupy Palestinian knafeh and ma'amoul, all detaining us for hours at the dining table. But this always gave us a chance to discuss how we would spend our time over the following days.

I try to emulate my mother's beautiful presentation of Christmas meals. She amassed a wonderful collection of festive hand-embroidered tablecloths, coasters, napkins, and decorations made by her talented late friend Rose Samaan, who was another mother figure to me. I treasure some of her unique Christmas designs that have been passed on to me, so full of memories. Mama also set the gold standard in Christmas tree design, with different rooms lit up magically in coordinated colours.

My family has always been spread around the globe, so one of the greatest Christmas treats would be having the time to catch up with those who had been abroad for work or studies or were visiting from afar.

When I was young, Bethlehem did not feel as hemmed in as it does now. There was no tall grey concrete wall nor were there Israeli checkpoints. So it was natural for us to go on Christmas outings to Jerusalem, just a few miles away. After all, my cousins and I went there every day for school. Going to the American Colony, a historic boutique hotel, gave the holiday a classic European flavour. For years, the hotel had a Swiss chef who offered a traditional Western Christmas menu—complete with cranberry sauce. I remember he also made a delectable German barley and bacon soup and spicy cinnamon Swiss cookies. The real highlight for us as children was the Christmas tree that was set up by the reception area with a train made out of gingerbread and the complimentary cookies.

A trip to Jericho—an hour or so away by car—could be desirable in winter because of its warmer clime. We would head to our family's favourite restaurant, Al Rawda. In December, the weather is mild, and you can sit outdoors at long wooden tables with an indulgent spread of Palestinian mezzeh (appetizers) and grilled meats while sipping tart, sugary lemonade and refreshing arak. After eating so many sugary cakes and biscuits over Christmas, it was always a healthy contrast to be able to nibble on fresh fruits—the miniature bananas, ripe oranges, mandarins, and tangerines that thrive in Jericho.

During the Christmas period other meals between feasts could always be constructed from leftovers. My love for kmaj bread (pita) was only enhanced by its usefulness as a pocket slathered with butter to savour cold meats with a smudge of mustard. Then, of course, thanks to the double hit of Christmas holidays in Bethlehem, the feasts would keep coming. No sooner were the Catholic Christmas dates over than we would have yet more generous invitations to special lunches and gatherings from our Orthodox family members.

QIDREH

This lamb and rice dish is the quintessential centerpiece for family celebrations in Palestine. Many will spice the meat and rice and then send it off to the wood-fired oven, where the ingredients are placed in a copper pot to cook slowly, releasing the flavours of garlic and coating the rice with the richness of the lamb meat.

MEAT

2 to 3 tablespoons extra-virgin olive oil

2 kg / 8¾ pounds bone-in lamb shoulder roast, cut in 2 cm / ¾-inch-thick slices of approximately 250 g / 9 ounces each

2 bay leaves

4 cardamom pods

1 cinnamon stick

1 onion, halved

1 tablespoon coarse sea salt

2 L / 2 quarts water

RICE AND CHICKPEAS

2½ tablespoons ghee or clarified butter

1 tablespoon extra-virgin olive oil

1 onion, finely chopped

10 to 12 peeled garlic cloves

1 teaspoon ground allspice

1 teaspoon ground turmeric

¼ teaspoon ground cumin

¼ teaspoon ground cardamom

¼ teaspoon ground coriander

¼ teaspoon ground cinnamon

¼ teaspoon ground nutmeg

500 g / 2½ cups medium-grain rice

250 g / 1½ cups dried chickpeas, soaked overnight and drained

GARNISH

½ teaspoon extra-virgin olive oil

60 g / ½ cup slivered almonds

60 g / ½ cup pine nuts

SERVES 6 TO 8

To prepare the meat, in a large pot, heat 2 tablespoons of the olive oil over medium-high heat and brown the meat on all sides, 5 to 8 minutes. You may have to work in batches, adding the additional 1 tablespoon oil as needed. Add the bay leaves, cardamom pods, cinnamon stick, onion, and salt. Add the water and bring to a boil. Decrease the heat and cook for 1½ to 2 hours, until the meat is tender.

Transfer the meat to a plate, strain the broth into a bowl, and discard the solids.

To prepare the rice and chickpeas, in a large pot, heat the ghee and olive oil over medium heat. Add the onion and cook until golden, 3 to 5 minutes. Add the garlic and sauté for 1 to 2 minutes. Add the allspice, turmeric, cumin, cardamom, coriander, cinnamon, and nutmeg and sauté for 1 minute. Stir in the rice and chickpeas. Add 1 L/ 4¼ cups of the strained lamb broth, bring to a boil over high heat, then decrease the heat to medium-low.

Cover the pot and leave to cook until the broth is absorbed, about 45 minutes. Add the meat to the pot with the rice and chickpeas and set aside for 10 minutes.

To prepare the garnish, in a small frying pan, heat the olive oil over medium heat. Add the almonds and toast for 3 minutes. Add the pine nuts and toast for 1 minute more, until golden.

Transfer the rice and meat to a serving tray and sprinkle with the toasted almonds and pine nuts.

ROASTED PORK LEG

With its large Christian population, Bethlehem has always had pig farms. In the beginning of the twentieth century, lamb became extremely expensive as a result of a disease affecting young sheep. Therefore, many people started raising pigs at home to capitalize on the high prices of pork. However, in what became known locally as "the crisis of pigs", the market was soon saturated and a big crash followed, leaving many people seriously out of pocket. Still, pork remains a popular part of our cuisine. I grew up with my mother making a fantastic ham for Christmas, my father loves pork chops, and I can always tempt visitors with a roasted pork leg.

1 tablespoon coriander
    seeds
1 tablespoon dried sage
2 teaspoons coarse sea salt
1 teaspoon dried rosemary
1 teaspoon dried zaatar
1 teaspoon freshly ground
    black pepper
1 teaspoon ground cumin
240 ml / 1 cup extra-virgin
    olive oil
2 whole garlic bulbs
1 bone-in pork leg, about
    3 kg / 6½ pounds
4 onions

SERVES 8

The night before you plan to roast the pork, make a rub. In a mortar, combine the coriander seeds, sage, salt, rosemary, zaatar, pepper, and cumin. Use the pestle to crush and mix well. Add 120 ml / ½ cup of the olive oil to end up with a paste.

Peel the cloves of one garlic bulb. Add to the mortar and crush into the paste.

Spread some parchment paper on the work top and rub the paste all over the pork. Cover the leg with the paper, put it on a baking sheet, and refrigerate overnight.

The next day, preheat the oven to its highest setting, usually 260°C / 500°F.

Pour the remaining 120 ml / ½ cup olive oil into a roasting pan. Cut the remaining garlic bulb in half horizontally and the onions into quarters. Add to the roasting pan. Lay the pork leg on top, fat-side up. Roast for 30 to 35 minutes, until the top is crackling.

Decrease the heat to 160°C / 325°F and roast for another 3½ to 4 hours. The meat is done when it is falling apart. Remove the pan from the oven and cover with aluminum foil.

Scrape all the juices and the fat into a small pot and heat on medium-low until the juices have reduced by half. Off the heat, squeeze the roasted garlic cloves out into the pot and use a hand blender to blend the sauce.

Place the pork leg on a board, and drizzle the sauce on top.

LAMB TESTICLES WITH SPICY TAHINIA

Traditionally, in Palestine, all parts of an animal were eaten. However, the way we consume meat today has changed. Sadly, we often look for the same cut of meat rather than celebrating the whole offering that nature gives us. All the offal and little-known cuts can be enjoyed with different cooking methods, providing varied flavors. Very often in Palestine, we grill offal. This recipe includes the sautéing of testicles. Arak is a high-alcohol anise-flavored spirit.

2 lamb testicles
1 tablespoon extra-virgin
   olive oil
120 ml / ½ cup arak
Juice of half a lemon
1 tablespoon coarse
   sea salt

SPICY TAHINIA
SAUCE
2 tablespoons tahinia
2 tablespoons warm water
1 tablespoon fresh lemon
   juice
1 garlic clove
½ red chilli pepper

SERVES 2

Ask the butcher to prepare the lamb testicles. If that's not possible, with a small knife, cut the outside skin and remove the outside layer. Soak the testicles in cold water for 15 to 20 minutes. Dry them well, then slice them in half lengthwise.

In a nonstick pan, heat the olive oil over medium-high heat. Add the testicles and sauté for about 2 minutes per side. Carefully add the arak to the pan; the alcohol will ignite. Let it burn off, then add the lemon juice and sprinkle with the salt. Make sure the meat has all gone white and there are no pink sides, but it is still moist. Then it is ready to serve.

To prepare the spicy tahinia sauce, combine the tahinia, water, lemon juice, garlic, and chilli pepper in a blender and process until smooth.

Serve the testicles with the sauce.

FALAFEL

Falafel is an essential Palestinian street food. You can find it on the corner of every street at every time of the day, offered both in little restaurants and by street vendors. Worldwide, it has become a vegan snack par excellence.

The best falafel for me are made at Afteem's, a restaurant in Bethlehem that specializes in falafel, houmous, musabaha, and ful. The Salameh family, owners of Afteem, were expelled from Jaffa in 1948 by Israel. Having arrived in Bethlehem as refugees, their grandfather sought a livelihood and opened a little stall making falafel on Star Street. They quickly built a reputation for making the best falafel in town. Since then, the restaurant has grown into three locations, and the secret to their success is both their recipes and the fact that they concentrate on making only a few key dishes they are known for.

I started making falafel during the pandemic, when under lockdown there was no way to indulge in the delightful houmous and falafel of Afteem.

160 g / 1 cup dried chickpeas, soaked in water to cover overnight and drained
20 g / ½ cup flat-leaf parsley, leaves and stems, finely chopped
20 g / ½ cup fresh coriander (cilantro) leaves and stems, finely chopped
½ onion
2 garlic cloves
1 teaspoon ground cumin
1 teaspoon ground coriander
½ teaspoon salt
½ teaspoon baking soda
½ tablespoon chickpea flour (optional)
Water (optional)
Vegetable oil, for frying

TO SERVE
Houmous Mutabal bil Tahinia (page 18)
Shawarma (page 126)
Tahinia Sauce (page 126)
Green Shatta (page 76)

MAKES 20 FALAFEL

Grind the chickpeas in a food processor. Add the parsley, fresh coriander, onion, garlic, cumin, ground coriander, salt, and baking soda to the food processor and process until you have a consistency that is close to the texture of wet sand but still a bit coarse.

Transfer the mixture to a bowl, cover, and refrigerate for 30 minutes.

If the mixture is too wet to form into patties, add the chickpea flour. If it's too dry to hold together, add a couple of teaspoons of water.

The best way to form the falafels is to use a falafel scooper, which you can find online. Alternatively, you can form them by hand. Form balls of the falafel mixture, then flatten them a bit so the sides are thinner than the centre. Place on a baking sheet.

Into a deep frying pan, pour about 8 cm / 3 inches of vegetable oil and heat to 180°C / 350°F.

Working in batches, slide the falafel patties into the hot oil and fry for 1 to 2 minutes, until they turn golden on the outside and are cooked on the inside. Scoop them out with a spider or slotted spoon, and drain on paper towels.

Serve the falafel with houmous, shawarma, tahinia dip, and shatta. *Sahtain!*

BUKJET RUZ

The Arabic word *bukja* means "parcel", and like *aumônière* in French, it is also used for food parcels. The use of filo pastry as a wrap was common in my Teta Julia's kitchen. She used to make these beautiful rounded bukjas filled with rice, peas, and meat. I remember cracking them open to let the steam come out with all the flavours and spices. We always had them with yoghurt on the side.

2 tablespoons extra-virgin olive oil
1 onion, finely chopped
3 garlic cloves, crushed
1 teaspoon salt
½ teaspoon ground black pepper
¼ teaspoon ground cinnamon
½ teaspoon ground allspice
¼ teaspoon ground nutmeg
¼ teaspoon ground cardamom
500 g / 18 ounces lamb, cut in cubes
400 g / 2 cups long-grain rice
250 g / 2 cups fresh green peas (or substitute frozen peas)
830 to 950 ml / 3½ to 4 cups water
1 tablespoon unsalted butter, melted
A pack filo pastry sheets
60 g / ½ cup almond slivers

SERVES 6 TO 8

Heat 1 tablespoon of the olive oil in a large pot over medium-high heat. Add the onion and sauté for 4 to 5 minutes, until translucent. Add the garlic, salt, pepper, cinnamon, allspice, nutmeg, and cardamom and give them a swirl to release their aroma. Add the lamb cubes and sauté them for at least 10 minutes, until they're coloured on all sides and cooked through.

Meanwhile, soak the rice in water to cover for a few minutes. Drain and rinse with water a few times until the water runs clear. Add the rice and the peas to the meat. Add enough of the water to cover the rice and a generous pinch of salt.

Bring to a boil, then decrease the heat to low, cover the pot, and cook until all of the water is absorbed and the rice is tender, about 25 minutes.

Take the pot off the heat, keep it covered, and leave it to rest for 10 minutes.

Pour the contents of the pot onto a large tray, and fluff the rice and the meat with a fork to allow it to cool down all the way through.

Preheat the oven to 180°C / 350°F. Combine the melted butter and the remaining 1 tablespoon olive oil in a small bowl. Brush the inside of a soup bowl with some of the butter/oil mixture.

Cut the filo pastry sheets to be long enough to line the bowl and fold over the filling. Line the bowl with three to four layers of stacked filo sheets and brush each sheet lightly with the butter/oil mixture. Fill the bowl with the cooled rice mixture, leaving a bit of space at the top. Fold the filo sheets to cover the rice with the three or four layers and brush it with butter/oil.

Line a baking sheet with parchment paper.

Flip the bowl onto the sheet to dislodge the bukja. Repeat the process to make 6 to 8 bukjas. Brush them again once they are all on the prepared baking sheet.

Bake for about 30 minutes, until the dough is crispy and golden. Serve hot.

CHRISTMAS EVE WITH TETA JULIA

While Christmas is an annual highlight for many people around the world, naturally in Bethlehem, it is something extra special. It can feel like the little town is always building up to this holiday. But these days, someone important is missing: my grandmother. Teta Julia truly loved Christmas, an occasion for so many things that she cared deeply about: flavoursome food, generous hospitality, charitable giving, the preservation of traditions, and, of course, big family get-togethers.

My grandmother Julia was the principal inspiration for my passion for cooking as a boy. I spent a lot of time at her house, absorbing her busy daily routine. There would always be enticing smells and a frenzy of activity in the kitchen as meals were prepared, often for guests. Meanwhile, farmers would call directly at the front door to offer their seasonal specialities: ripe prickly pears, watermelons from Jenin, fat courgettes (zucchini), and finger-length aubergines (eggplant) from Battir.

The days started early, and often by 10 in the morning, my grandmother would be patiently waiting on the terrace for a friend to attend an event at the Arab Women's Union, where she was one of the founders. To my delight, women coming to see her from neighbouring villages would often bear tasty gifts: sweet dibs (grape molasses) from Khirbet Beit Zakariyyah or honey from Ubeidiya, and salty laban jameed (salted and dried yoghurt) from local Bedouin communities.

As Christmas approached, my grandparents' home would bustle excitedly with energy. My grandmother had been raised in a home where Christmas traditions were hugely important. They had been ingrained in her by her father, my great-grandfather, Mattia Kattan, whom she described compellingly in her book, *Lest We Forget*. Sadly, he died before I was born, but I appreciated that he was the well-travelled, multilingual son of a former mayor of Bethlehem, a merchant with shops in Amman, Haifa, and Jerusalem, who was dedicated to his large family. He was the loving father of eight girls—an accomplished lineup which included both my grandmothers—and one boy.

My grandmother took huge pride in our city and always strove to preserve its stories and memories for locals as well as its many international visitors. This can clearly be seen in the Beituna al-Talhami Museum which was established by the Arab Women's Union under her administration and through her record of community work. Long before December 24, Christmas Eve for our Catholic family, she and her friends would be knitting sweaters to be sent as Christmas gifts to Palestinian political prisoners in Israeli jails. There were always charitable fund-raising activities and Christmas parties for the less well-off in our community to organise, too.

My grandmother instilled in all her grandchildren the values of solidarity and philanthropy. My siblings, cousins, and I were always encouraged to think of those less fortunate than ourselves, particularly in the run-up to Christmas. We would make small donations from our pocket money to local charities, including the orphanages, so that the children cared for there could have a Christmas gift and a festive meal.

Our family's Christmas preparations have always begun in earnest on December 1, the start of Advent, which also happens to be my birthday. From this date on, Christmas trees and decorations are on display, Christmas carols can be legitimately played, and stacks of Julia's rich Christmas cake start building up. Funnily enough, the recipe for the cake was simply based on an old Betty Crocker one, which Teta adapted to include locally sourced Palestinian ingredients, adding extra cinnamon and nutmeg, moist dates, fleshy dried apricots, and figs. Throughout December, Teta's home would be filled with this Christmassy smell. Her oven was on nonstop—and the kitchen was converted into a mini production line for her cakes.

I have no idea how many Christmas cakes Teta would make each year, but it was a lot. Most were devoured or handed out to loved ones just before Christmas. My main task as an enthusiastic young kitchen assistant was to chop the dried fruit and then coat the pieces in flour before adding them to the cake mix so they did not just slump down to the bottom of the baking tin. Sometimes I would also be trusted to lay out all the long rectangular cake pans and line them with parchment paper while my grandmother and her regular kitchen helper got the cake mix ready. Finally, as the cakes slowly baked, we would sit expectantly in the kitchen, keeping an eye on them. When my grandfather came home from work, the irresistible aroma would always put a smile on his face.

Nowadays, the Israeli state's construction of the segregation wall has marred one of the main highlights of Christmas celebrations—the procession of church officials from Jerusalem's Old City to the Nativity Church in Bethlehem. But when I was growing up, large crowds of joyful Christians, mostly from Bethlehem and the surrounding areas, would gather along the route to welcome the procession, with the first clusters at Mar Elias Monastery, on a hill at the edge of the city, and at Rachel's Tomb, where many notables would wait. As

my grandparents' house was well located along the route inside Bethlehem, we would congregate there in the front garden on December 24 to greet the Roman Catholic patriarch who heads the convoy and watch the scouts and horses who accompanied him. My grandparents—who had close relations with the church— were always ready to salute the patriarch of the day. After he had passed, we went inside for a grand lunch.

In the weeks leading up to this event, the conversation would revolve around whom to invite to the lunch. My grandmother, the generous hostess, hated to leave anyone out and always secretly invited extra guests. She would also welcome those who had not been invited as we packed inside. By now, the exquisitely decorated Christmas tree would be ready with gifts wrapped for everyone so that for us children, this was always an exhilarating time. Despite extensive conversations among the family about what our lunch should involve, the menu was usually more or less the same.

The appetisers were invariably sfiha (meat-filled flatbreads), sambousek (crispy meat pies), kibbeh (spiced meat and bulgur wheat), and a local salad.

Then my grandmother would make what she called "Oriental rice", on which she lavished minced meat (ground meat), festive grilled chestnuts, almonds, and pine nuts. This would accompany roasted turkey and a roasted lamb shank as well as her famous glazed carrots. Some years, she would opt for a whole roasted lamb stuffed with rice and meat. It was always an epic meal. On these occasions, many of my relatives would shy away from the head of the lamb, but Teta would cut this and quietly serve it to those of us privileged to know the value of the delicacy and sometimes to others who had no idea what it was. I would contentedly tuck into the brain meat, bone marrow, and any other parts of the lamb, leaving others to enjoy the leaner but, in my opinion, less tasty meat.

I am eternally grateful that I had such exceptional grandparents and that I was able to spend so much time with Teta Julia. She taught me about every Palestinian spice and herb, and most importantly, about Palestinian hospitality, the love of Bethlehem, and the importance of resilience.

Teta's Christmas lunches, her pièces de résistances, would always end with her Christmas cake. We were only allowed to taste it for the first time on Christmas Eve. There was a ritual in which she took a cake out of the refrigerator, where it would have been stored for three weeks, for us to slice it together. After so much anticipation, that first taste was always a memorable moment.

After Teta Julia passed away, the entire family was in denial, but Christmastime was the hardest, the time when her absence was most painful. It took me several years to realise that I could bake her Christmas cake and share it with the family in her memory, as a tribute to her.

A glorious Christmas Eve lunch would taper off rather than end. Then we would sit around, our stomachs full, sipping Arabic coffee, and our attention would begin to shift to midnight Mass. While much of the family would be heading to the Nativity Church, the scramble for the sought-after tickets, which had often begun in the autumn, was off-putting for my grandmother. Instead, along with my grandfather and parents, she preferred to head to the chapel at Bethlehem University, another eminent local institution which she had helped to found.

TETA JULIA'S CHRISTMAS CAKE

Beginning December 1, my grandparents' house would be filled with the aroma of Christmas cake, my grandmother's adaptation of a traditional fruitcake recipe that includes her personal Palestinian touch.

This cake symbolizes Christmas for all of us in the family, as Teta Julia would share the love and fill up all our refrigerators with loaves of it.

After her passing, it was a while before I had the courage to revive the ritual. Now, not a Christmas passes by without my baking her famous cake.

4 whole eggs
200 g / 1 cup sugar
240 ml / 1 cup
   vegetable oil
170 g / ½ cup dibs (grape
   molasses)
240 ml / 1 cup orange juice
420 g / 3½ cups all-
   purpose flour
2 teaspoons ground
   cinnamon
1 teaspoon baking powder
1 teaspoon salt
1 teaspoon ground nutmeg
1 teaspoon ground allspice
1 teaspoon ground ginger
1 teaspoon ground
   cardamom
480 g / 2 cups dates,
   pitted and quartered
280 g / 2 cups raisins
100 g / 1 cup walnut pieces
90 g / ½ cup dried
   apricots, halved
80 g / ½ cup dried
   figs, halved
70 g / ½ cup dried
   cherries

YIELDS 1 LOAF CAKE

Preheat the oven to 150°C / 300°F. Line a 23 by 13 cm / 9 by 5-inch loaf pan with aluminum foil, making sure the foil overhangs the edges of the pan. Line the foil with parchment paper, making sure the parchment also overhangs the edges.

In a large mixing bowl, beat the eggs with the sugar until light. Mix in the oil and molasses. Add the orange juice.

In a separate bowl, whisk together 280 g / 2 cups of the flour, the cinnamon, baking powder, salt, nutmeg, allspice, ginger, and cardamom. Add the dry ingredients to the wet and mix gently until you have a smooth batter.

In another bowl, combine the dates, raisins, walnuts, apricots, figs, and cherries with the remaining 140 g / 1 cup flour. Toss to coat well.

Put the dried fruit mixture in the prepared pan and pour the batter over. Set aside to allow the batter to sink in well around the mixture, about 15 minutes.

Bake, uncovered, for 1 hour. Check the cake with a toothpick; if the cake is liquid but browning on top, fold the parchment paper and foil to seal the cake and continue baking for 30 minutes.

Place the pan on a wire rack to cool completely. Wrap the cake well in the parchment and foil and store in the refrigerator for at least 1 week before enjoying it.

ACKNOWLEDGEMENTS

Writing this book has been a journey of introspection, fun, culinary delights, historical exploration and much more.

I would like to thank every person who has knowingly or unknowingly supported me in this process.

Special thanks to those who have left me with their memories, stories, and love; thank you Teta Julia, Sido Michel, Teta Emily, and Sido Nakhleh.

Thanks to my wonderful family for putting up with me, encouraging me, and providing criticism like only you can— for tasting the dishes, inspiring recipes, and for all the love!

Thanks to the team at Hardie Grant, and a thank-you to for Jenny Wapner, publisher extraordinaire. She demonstrated skills of patience that still baffle me.

Thank you to the partners and teams at Fawda, Akub, Kassa, and the Wonder Cabinet. You are the ones that make it happen, every day!

A very special thank-you to each person in this book—each artisan, farmer, restaurateur—you're all stars! Not only would this book not exist without you, none of my cooking would. You infuse the *nafas* into this journey.

Thanks to the iconic Gemma Bell for having believed in me from the first day she pushed open that door at Hosh Al-Syrian years ago.

Thank you to the great tetas and the team at the Palestine Institute for Public Diplomacy for the great adventure that was filming *Teta's Kitchen*.

Thank you to everyone who has dined with us, watched the shows, and written about Palestinian food. Thank you for your stories, your support, and your feedback, always.

Thank you to every mother, father, grandmother, grandfather, chef, and cook, at home, or in a restaurant, who cooks Palestinian food and transmits the love of Palestinian food. You are the real heroes who preserve our cuisine and share our hospitality with the world.

INDEX

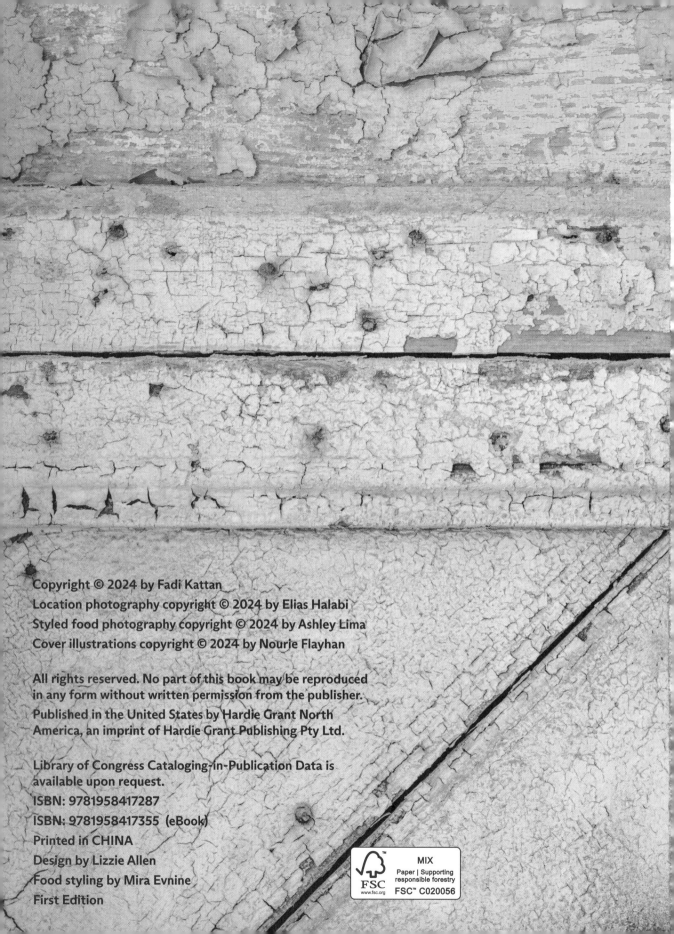

Published in the United States by Hardie Grant North
America, an imprint of Hardie Grant Publishing Pty Ltd.

Library of Congress Cataloging-in-Publication Data is
available upon request.
ISBN: 9781958417287
ISBN: 9781958417355 (eBook)
Printed in CHINA
Design by Lizzie Allen
Food styling by Mira Evnine
First Edition

MIX
Paper | Supporting
responsible forestry
FSC
www.fsc.org   FSC™ C020056